Traditionally Fermented Foods

Innovative Recipes and
Old-Fashioned Techniques
for Sustainable Eating

Shannon Stonger

founder of Nourishing Days and writer for Cultures for Health

PAGE STREET
PUBLISHING CO.

PAGE STREET
PUBLISHING CO.

First published in 2017 by
Page Street Publishing Co.
27 Congress Street, Suite 105
Salem, MA 01970
www.pagestreetpublishing.com

Distributed by Macmillan, sales in Canada by The Canadian Manda Group.

20 19 18 17   1 2 3 4

ISBN-13: 978-1-62414-330-4
ISBN-10: 1-62414-330-X

Library of Congress Control Number: 2016957529

Cover and book design by Page Street Publishing Co.
Photography by Shannon Stonger

Printed and bound in China

Page Street is proud to be a member of 1% for the Planet. Members donate one percent of their sales to one or more of the over 1,500 environmental and sustainability charities across the globe who participate in this program.

For Cynthia, for your friendship and for telling me,
in no uncertain terms, to write a book.

Contents

Grains / 69

Dairy / 117

Beverages / 161

Condiments / 193

Introduction

When the food we ate tasted of the soil from which it came, there were no large freezers to keep our food in for the winter. When able bodies were needed to work the land, true nourishment from the food on your plate was one of your most valuable resources. And when laundry was washed by hand, gardens needed planting and water was heated on the wood stove, fermentation was a part of the everyday workings of a traditional food(s) kitchen.

This sounds like the pioneer storybooks of our childhood, but it is also my reality, or at least part of it. For at least twelve years now, I have known that I wanted to—and needed to, really—pursue what is commonly called homesteading. For ten of those years, both on- and off-grid, I have been practicing what has become an invaluable tool in our homestead kitchen: fermentation.

As a newlywed, I hesitantly put a bowl of milk inoculated with a bit of yogurt into a pilot-lit oven. Eight hours later it wobbled its way into my refrigerator. Homemade yogurt soon became a weekly mainstay that aided us in pinching pennies—so that we could pay off student loans; so that we could buy a couple of acres of land.

A year later, I felt more of a push to get away from industrialized foods and embrace local food culture and a DIY lifestyle. Not surprisingly, this sudden conviction coincided with the birth of our first child, as these things often do.

And so I began fermenting farmers' market vegetables and storing them in half-gallon jugs in our refrigerator, bringing together my desires for nourishing traditional foods and local, homegrown foods. We planted our first garden in the backyard of a rental. I hung laundry with a baby in a sling, dirt under my fingernails and kefir smoothies fueling my morning.

Defining Sustainability

Throughout this book and on my blog, I often use the word sustainable. *In our green-washed lexicon,* sustainable *has ecological ties. It is environmentally friendly. It is natural. And for me, personally, it is the antithesis to the industrialized food system and the way of life that fuels such an entity.*

I also subscribe to the other meaning of the word; in fact, I think the two are inextricably intertwined. Being sustainable means that something is repeatable. It is a practice or a way of life that can be maintained in the long term, generation after generation. In order for a way of life, a practice or a food to be so, it must be moderate, both in its demands on resources and its demands of time and energy from those performing the act.

True sustainability, in my mind, is not a big push for greener products nor a vast movement for change. It is in the small and seemingly mundane tasks and needs of everyday life. It is in where our food comes from, the way we choose to feed our families and how we teach our children to live.

The more in touch I became with the land, the more fermentation seemed an outpouring of my desire to give our children a more sustainable way of life. It became a tool that I would come to use more and more when we finally made the jump to live off-grid.

Sourdough baking, milk kefir making and kombucha brewing all became a regular part of my week. I was at home raising babies while continuing my lifelong interest in science. Many thought my chemistry degree was going unused but I was harnessing food chemistry to benefit our health and forward our homestead dreams. To this day I am amazed at how fermentation weaves together the threads of my life.

Eventually we did move off-grid, though we are not the *Little House on the Prairie* homesteaders you may envision. We are somewhere between where we were and where we'd like to be, chopping firewood and hauling water one minute, running laptops and the Internet off of solar panels the next. We buy weekly groceries and order bulk grains online; make kefir from our goat milk and ferment okra pickles from our garden.

Our reality, when juxtaposed with our goals, makes the simple life seem like a misnomer.

I try to remember that these things are not built in a day; that starting from scratch may mean our generation will see few of the benefits our children will. Mostly, we just try to keep planting and fermenting with the hope that the heritage we leave is one of proper stewardship.

I get asked a lot by those who read the Nourishing Days blog about the "why" behind the life that we've chosen. A cookbook could not encompass all of those reasons, nor should it. But I will attempt to share one of these reasons as it pertains to food and agriculture.

It is estimated that approximately 2 percent of the population of the nation I inhabit practices some form of agriculture. And yet the other 98 percent of us must eat, too. That this fact is startling to me is an understatement; that the fruit of this is large corporations controlling our food system and poisoning our children for profit cannot come as a surprise. I believe this is the price we are paying for becoming that 98 percent.

To eat is to, in no small way, take from the land. How we take from the land, and whether or not we give back to it, is the ignorance we live in when we are the 98 percent. This is one of the ways in which this agrarian life chose us, not the other way around. When I consider our five young children and the heritage we leave them, I see no other options.

The problems with industrial agriculture are too big to beat, I am told, when I talk to folks of all walks of life—both those of the agrarian persuasion and those who are not. I agree, we may have passed the point where political acts as we know them can make a dent in such a rolling stone as this.

And yet, I think we all know what is needed—more hands in the dirt, more heirloom seeds being planted, more home dairies, more families raising and growing their own food. And certainly less buying from corporations who will pillage our land without consideration of the consequences to the generations to come.

No, rallies and ballot boxes will not make *the* difference. But I can almost guarantee that when we stop buying from and financially supporting the very entities and ideas we know are wrong, things will shift ... starting with our own hearts ... if only we are willing to take on the work.

And so it is that a simple jar of kimchi, crafted from garden produce, or a glass of homegrown goat kefir has been my stand against big agriculture; my form of kitchen activism. I cannot change the hearts and acts of men, but I can certainly take responsibility for my own.

Fermentation, with its long tradition of sustaining those who have toiled on the land, has been both a tool and a gift to me as I have walked the path of these convictions.

My desire, in the pages of this book, is to pass that gift on to you.

Shannon Stonger

The Basic Fermentation Process

While I see fermentation as an art easily adapted to one's individual needs, it is only as valuable and flexible as our understanding of the process is thorough. That is to say, if we want to use this tool to its fullest potential, we best start by knowing how it works.

Fermented foods are as old as food itself. They harness simple biological processes to create food that is both preserved and bettered by the act. In a world in which most of the man-made processes actually degrade the natural goodness of a food or require a great deal of man-made resources to preserve it, fermentation is a refreshing alternative.

The process of fermentation is a simple one. Microorganisms exist everywhere, including on the food we eat and in the air we breathe. Vegetables and grains receive a dose of bacteria from their growth in the soil. Raw dairy products contain a host of beneficial organisms. These can be harnessed by giving them the correct environment in which to flourish. There is a fork in the road that all foods must take. One path leads toward a complete decomposition in which the food returns to the land. The other takes a pit stop, not only preserving itself into something edible but something that is actually good for the human body. This second path is called fermentation.

A good example of this is vegetable fermentation. A cucumber has its own microbial makeup from the soil in which it was grown. Place it in salt water at a temperature of anywhere between 50 and 80°F (10 and 26°C), and not long after that, bacteria will begin to multiply. While these bacteria multiply, an acid called lactic acid is produced. This is where the term *lacto-fermentation* comes from; it does not refer to the inclusion of whey or dairy, as is sometimes assumed. Rather it is a reference to the type of bacteria being multiplied and the resulting lactic acid, which preserves the food.

Eventually, your jar of cucumbers begins to bubble. This is because carbon dioxide is produced when the bacteria feast on simple sugars. It is a by-product of fermentation that comes in handy; it displaces the oxygen in a sealed vessel, thereby perpetuating the anaerobic environment needed for proper vegetable fermentation.

At this point you have a good number of bacteria—primarily lactic acid bacteria. You have organic acids—mostly lactic acid but also acetic acid (vinegar). You may also have a bit of yeast on the surface of the brine, which is normal and fine as long as it doesn't take over.

This same process applies to grains when you make a sourdough starter. Mix grain and water and introduce oxygen. At first bacteria multiply and seemingly take over but, due to the oxygen and simple sugars, yeasts begin to proliferate and eventually you have a symbiotic culture containing both bacteria and yeast. Carbon dioxide is produced during the fermentation process, which then raises the bread.

Similar processes take place when you make yogurt, milk kefir, kombucha, sauerkraut and more.

This process is both beautiful and technical. It is a process that can preserve vegetables and dairy and make bread digestible and light. And it does it all while predigesting the food and adding the enzymes, probiotics and vitamins that make the final fermented product better for the human body than the raw food you began with.

It is really quite miraculous.

FERMENTED FOODS IN FOOD PRESERVATION

Much of the modern rhetoric surrounding fermented foods is simply about getting more probiotic foods into our bodies. This is a great example of using food as medicine to close the cycle between man and land. But it is only one side of the coin.

We live in a time of plenty, where the options are many and the truly hard times few. In times when we depended completely on the land and the work of our hands for survival, the concept of probiotics was not yet part of the rhetoric. Even if it was, it would be at the bottom of the list of food preservation priorities.

I believe, however, that our ancestors knew intuitively that fermented foods were not only preserving their food but were doing it in a way that helped them to make it through the months in which nothing fresh was to be found. They must have known, from the bubbling kraut and tangy kefir, that fermented foods were alive.

And so I look at fermentation as multifaceted. It is a means of food preservation. It is a way to get more living foods into my family. It is medicine and sustenance and sustainability rolled into one. In that light, sometimes I ferment a great deal of garden vegetables—and sometimes I choose other forms of food preservation.

Fermenting vs. Canning

If you have previously preserved your harvest through canning, fermentation may seem like an enigma. In fermentation, you don't want to add vinegar, boiling is bad practice and leaving jars unattended for years isn't the ideal way to look at it.

Instead of a one-and-done, fermentation is a process. There is the initial intense period of fermentation that often happens at room temperature, but you do not then simply move things to cold storage and forget about them. Things can change in those jars you've stashed away, which is why old texts suggest that you check on the sauerkraut that happens to be sitting right next to the bushel of apples in the cellar.

I therefore find it detrimental to proclaim lacto-fermentation as a complete replacement for canning. For one, the processes are completely different and should be distinguished as such. More importantly, though, there is a place for both in sustainable food preservation.

For instance, I do not ferment vegetables during the hottest summer months here in Texas. It's simply too hot to ensure a safe fermentation that would preserve the vegetables for long-term food storage. Instead, I choose dehydration and then canning—in that order—to put food up. Then when the fall garden comes on, I return to fermenting whatever produce we grow or find locally or on sale at grocery stores to supply us with a good stock of krauts and pickles for the few winter months we endure.

Depending on your climate, you can layer fermentation into other means of food preservation to make the very most of your food. Ferment first (for health reasons) and then choose dehydration, canning or freezing, depending on your circumstances. Putting all of your preserved foods in that single proverbial basket just doesn't make good sense.

What does work is prioritizing. I ferment first, if possible, because ferments are living foods. I dehydrate second because this requires almost no resources in our dry climate. I also can when I have used the first two techniques and still have more to preserve for long-term storage. Of course, I am primarily speaking of vegetables, which can be preserved for long-term storage through fermentation.

Dairy, grains and fruits can also be preserved in the short-term by simple lactic acid fermentation. Turning milk into milk kefir will give you a predictably sour milk that can sit on the counter for several days. Sourdough bread keeps much longer than its store-bought counterpart due to the acidity in the dough. Fruits can be fermented using lactic acid methods, but they turn to alcohol in the long term, so dehydration, canning and winemaking are better long-term food preservation methods.

The Things I Don't Ferment

I have fermented just about everything you can imagine, usually deliberately, sometimes not. After much trial and error and keeping practicality at the forefront on our little homestead, there are foods I simply choose not to ferment. Fruits are one of them. We eat them fresh or dehydrate them if they make it past greedy little hands. I occasionally make something like Fermented Pear and Ginger Sauce (page 201) for short-term shelf life extension. If I were ever to have a huge windfall, making wine makes more sense than lactic acid fermentation anyway.

Beans are another food I generally don't ferment. I will soak beans for a good long while, sometimes approaching fermentation, but we generally don't go out of our way to ferment them before or after cooking. We do, however, often eat ferments with these foods—fruit with cultured dairy, beans with all sorts of fermented vegetables, sourdough breads and fermented hot sauces, for instance.

Fermentation makes a lot of sense most of the time, but not all of the time.

FERMENTED FOODS AS MEDICINE

The adage "Let food be thy medicine" is revolutionary in times such as this. When more than 90 percent of the food available in supermarkets is more of a toxin than a tonic, you know that we are fighting an uphill battle.

And yet, like so many other things, we need only look backward to find real, lasting solutions. "Eat old food," I've often heard; the things your great-grandmother would have eaten. How many generations will we have to go back before we realize how broken this one is?

Old foods contain a memory of the seed, the soil beneath calloused hands or the face of an animal that was tended. Old food has roots, deeply planted in the traditions of cultures that survived on nothing at all fancy or year-round, but rather simple and seasonal. Old food and its methods were passed down out of the need for survival and nourishment. Fermented foods are old foods.

Using fermented foods as medicine became a reality for me when I realized that we truly are what we eat. I would even argue that, when consuming animal products, we are what we eat eats. The mysterious beauty of fermented foods is that they actually take the very bacteria from the soil that the food was grown in and multiply them in order to create lactic acid, thereby preserving the food. Man is but a catalyst by which the right environment takes place; he has yet to create a system as brilliantly holistic and sustainable as lactic acid fermentation.

Enzymes: The Forgotten Benefit of Fermented Foods

There is much talk about the probiotics in fermented foods and the many health benefits they bring. I'm a fan and have said so over and over again in this book. One thing I don't hear people talk a lot about, however, is the enzymatic quality of fermented foods.

We often think of raw fruits and vegetables as the biggest source of enzymes. Fermented versions of those foods, however, are like raw foods *enhanced* in that their vitamin count, enzymes and digestibility goes through the roof after going through a proper fermentation transformation. You are taking what is already good for you and giving it wings, so to speak.

Should Everyone Eat Fermented Foods?

I have heard from too many people who have trouble with all sorts of foods, including fermented ones, not to include this caveat. Over the years, almost everyone I have corresponded with about fermented foods seems to benefit from them. Almost everyone.

There are a very few with very severe health problems for whom fermented foods seem to trigger negative symptoms. From what I can tell, there could be three reasons for this:

- *They could be having a very strong die-off reaction. If dysbiosis, very low stomach acid or a chronic digestive issue is present, the body may have a very strong reaction to the influx of bacteria and yeast. In this case, fermented foods must be introduced very slowly.*

- *They could have a very sensitive or weakened immune or histamine response. For those with very severe issues of this type, certain wild fermentations, and the wild strains of bacteria and yeast that come with them, could initially cause undesirable symptoms. Sticking strictly to controlled cultured foods that are fermented in a sealed jar or within the confines of an airlock system may be their best bet.*

- *They may need to take other drastic measures to heal themselves before their bodies can handle the influx of living elements that fermented foods offer. In this case, they will need to work with a health-care professional to determine what treatments may be needed and what, if any, fermented or cultured foods they should consume.*

Not only that, but fermentation also aids in making sure that other foods cannot block enzymes. There are substances in all seeds—nuts, seeds, grains and beans—called enzyme inhibitors. These little guys do exactly what their name says: They inhibit the ability of enzymes to break down macronutrients, resulting in subpar digestion. Fermentation of grains and seeds neutralizes enzyme inhibitors.

It's also important to note that enzymes and probiotics play vastly different roles in our body's health and digestion. They are similar to the bacteria and yeast that tend to live in symbiosis in cultures such as sourdough or kombucha, in that they exist in harmony.

That is to say, both probiotics and enzymes are needful and, happily, both are present in fermented foods.

THE INCREDIBLE FLAVOR-BOOSTING QUALITY OF FERMENTED FOODS

While it is reason enough to make and consume fermented foods for their health benefits, their role in sustainable food systems and their simple nature, I argue for one more reason: They are not only delicious on their own but enhance any food they are made from or combined with.

Many foods and beverages touted as holding umami, the so-called fifth element of taste, are fermented. Soy sauce, fish sauce, fermented beverages and fermented vegetables all have it. It is a mouth sensation that seems so complex as to be unexplainable.

Fermentation creates umami when enzymes break proteins down into amino acids. These amino acids, specifically glutamate, create flavors otherwise unknown. And fermented foods do so with very little effort.

Eating Fermented Foods at Their Nutritional Peak

Biologically speaking, there is a sweet spot for all fermented foods. I touch on this briefly in the chapter on vegetables, but it is important to note that this applies to all raw, fermented foods.

Both probiotics and enzymes have environmental preferences. Under certain conditions they thrive and proliferate; under other conditions they peter out and die. One of those environmental factors is the pH or acidity of the fermented food. As the pH drops due to lactic acid production, bacteria and enzyme counts change.

It may be true that our stomachs are acidic enough to not allow certain microorganisms to pass through to the intestines. But it certainly doesn't hurt to maximize the benefits of your ferments by eating them at their prime.

If you are consuming fermented foods for these bacteria and enzymes, you need to know when they are at their optimal numbers. This sweet spot occurs after the food has had a chance to fully ferment but before it has consumed all of the fuel (lactose in milk, starches in vegetables and so forth) and turned too acidic.

Practically speaking, this looks like yogurt and kefir that have fermented for approximately 24 hours and are tangy but have not gone to firm curds and whey. This looks like fermented vegetables that still clearly have some life to them, having fermented for at least three to six weeks but not having a lackluster, deadened appearance. This looks like bubbly beverages whose vinegary notes are subtle, not overpowering. This looks like living, breathing, fermented foods.

Think about sourdough bread and how that tang gives it a complexity you really can't achieve with commercial yeast. Consider homebrewed kombucha whose sweet, tart flavor is difficult to come by commercially. Remember a well-aged cheese, a kimchi or a kraut that was fermented for just the right amount of time. The combination of heat, spice and tang creates something that is more than the sum of its parts.

And so these foods that are good for you, if made right and incorporated properly, can also be some of the most delicious you could ever come across. The recipes in this book are my attempt to showcase that flavor.

Fermented Foods vs. Cultured Foods

Many use the words fermented *and* cultured *interchangeably. While, indeed, they are both probiotic, enzyme-rich foods made through fermentation, there is one small but distinct difference.*

Cultured foods are generally made with what is known as a mother culture. These cultures are generally self-perpetuating—they are used to culture a food and then can either be reused or multiply themselves in a form that can be reused. This describes kombucha, milk kefir, yogurt and any fermented food made with the use of a culture starter. When these foods ferment, they are considered cultured in that they have been inoculated by a separate source of bacteria to sway the fermentation in a specific direction.

In contrast, wild fermentation utilizes naturally occurring bacteria on the surface of fruits and vegetables, in raw milk and on the surface of grains. These bacteria naturally proliferate under the right conditions, creating a fermented food teeming with bacteria given by the soil and air.

CULTURE CARE AND BEST PRACTICES

There are many principles in fermentation that apply to all fermented foods across the board. These general practices should be considered for the health and longevity of mother cultures and in troubleshooting specific ferments.

Aerobic vs. Anaerobic Ferments

While some fermented foods require a lack of oxygen to thrive, others need oxygen for the proliferation of the microorganisms to occur. Aerobic fermentation—that which occurs with oxygen—is often correlated with ferments that contain both bacteria and yeasts and ferments that contain a fair amount of acetic acid. Examples of aerobic fermentation include kombucha, water and milk kefir, and sourdough. Fermented vegetables are primarily anaerobic, while yogurt and milk kefir tend to have traits of both.

For anaerobic fermentation, you must use tight-fitting lids during the fermentation process to block out both oxygen and foreign microorganisms. In the case of fermented vegetables, an anaerobic environment is generally created using brine. For aerobic fermentation, the foods or liquids are given access to oxygen via a permeable lid that lets air in, but keeps bugs and debris out.

Spacing Cultures to Avoid Cross-Contamination

Cultures are incredibly resilient. Even when I think I have neglected them for too long or that they have been contaminated, I have seen mother cultures survive and come back strong, again and again. But there is no reason to be purposefully reckless or neglectful.

If you are keeping several types of aerobic cultures in your kitchen, then there is a small probability of the microorganisms of one crossing with another. This has the potential to change the microbial makeup of one of your ferments, thereby changing or ruining it.

The solution I tend to employ is to create fermentation zones. I keep sourdough, water kefir, milk kefir and kombucha in their own zone, at least a couple of feet apart in various parts of my kitchen. Fermented vegetables can be grouped with any of these aerobic ferments as they are generally fermented in sealed jars.

Taking a Break from or Preserving Mother Cultures

If keeping your cultures alive feels like a major burden, please know that you can put them aside for a short time or for the long term and come back to them later. Here are two methods to do so.

Short-Term Storage with Refrigeration

Milk kefir, water kefir, yogurt and sourdough can all be kept in the refrigerator in a fresh batch of their culturing medium (milk, flour or sugar water) for one to two weeks. After the storage period, you can take them out, refresh them and continue using them at room temperature, or you can feed them again and place them back into the refrigerator.

Long-Term/Off-Grid Storage

These same cultures can be stored for the long term through dehydration. By removing the moisture, you are essentially putting the bacteria into dormancy. The easiest way to keep milk kefir grains, water kefir grains or sourdough starter for the long term is to spread it thinly on a clean plate or dehydrator tray and allow it to dry below 118°F (48°C), as this is the temperature at which enzymes are killed. It can then be stored in a cool, dry place for six to twelve months.

Note that dehydration, much like forgetting a feeding or extremes in temperature, can be a stressor on a culture. It may not be quite so vital once you rehydrate it or it may take a bit of time to come back to life fully.

Kombucha SCOBYs (symbiotic colonies of bacteria and yeast) are a bit different in that they create, and can exist in, a much more acidic environment. For that reason, you can actually leave your kombucha SCOBY in the kombucha liquid and it will keep for weeks, and even months, due to the kombucha's low pH. Be sure there is enough liquid to cover the SCOBY; you will need to check your culture from time to time to make sure the liquid hasn't evaporated. You can store these vessels, sometimes referred to as SCOBY hotels, at room temperature.

Of Water and Salt: Choosing Common Fermentation Ingredients

These two lifebloods of the human diet are also the two most common ingredients to all areas of fermentation. As such, I'd like to take a moment to touch on how to choose water and salt sources for the recipes in this book.

Water seems as though it is a universal ingredient, but there are actually enough variations that some water choices can actually interfere with the fermentation process.

Any chemicals in water, predominantly chlorine, can interfere with the fermentation process. Consider the fact that chlorine bleach is used to kill bacteria in swimming pools and in housecleaning.

For that reason, I recommend using filtered water, if at all possible. This can be well water, municipal water or, in our case, rainwater. For all of these choices putting it through a high-quality filter is ideal. If this is not available to you, consider purchasing true spring water or leave your tap water uncovered on the counter overnight, a method some fermenters have found works to eliminate unwanted chlorine.

Salt is another basic ingredient, but the choices can be endless. All of the recipes in this book were tested with a fine-grained pink Himalayan or Celtic sea salt. Any unrefined sea or Himalayan salt works well. Refined table salt will work, in that it does the job of slowing down fermentation, preserving flavor and texture. It probably goes without saying that less refined is usually better.

Sugar Content of Final Ferments

A very common question about ferments is how much sugar is left in the final product. Because the fermentation process includes the consumption of the sugar by the bacteria and yeast, there is no way to say exactly without testing.

However, if sugar is a concern for you, you do have options. Most of the recipes have a range of fermentation time; for the lowest sugar content, you will want to let it ferment as long as it can before it runs completely out of food. This will always result in a tangier sourdough bread, yogurt, kraut, kefir and so forth. You can, therefore, let taste and time be your guide.

TROUBLESHOOTING MOLD: A FLOWCHART

Before you panic at the sight of something in the white, fuzzy or funky department, remember this: Yeasts and molds are everywhere. We inoculate cheese with some of the funkiest-looking stuff around, making it utterly delicious. Some of the tastiest sausages are covered in what we might call a white mold.

Not all mold is bad. Not all mold is yeast.

Yeasts are common in fermented foods and are desirable in aerobic ferments. Good bacteria and good yeasts can live in harmony to protect foods from *unwanted* strains of these microorganisms.

The key is not to panic and to know what to look for. Fuzz on top of your kefir might be fine. White yeast on your kraut could be expected. Textured something-or-other on your sourdough starter might not be worth getting worked up about. To illustrate this point, I want to show you something that often shows up on top of the kvasses I make.

The above-right photo shows what is often referred to as kahm yeast. It is a very thin layer of yeast that forms on the surface of ferments that have been exposed to oxygen. Very many of my jars of vegetable ferments have, upon opening, developed a layer of this if they have not been consumed within a week or two. Heat tends to bring this on more readily. I have also seen it on milk kefir and sourdough starter that have tasted and cultured just fine.

Please don't freak out and throw out whatever fermented food you found with this stuff on top! Unless you see some of the signs to worry about that I will describe shortly, it is fine. It is normal for yeast to develop in moist, oxygen-rich environments. Scrape it off your vegetable ferment, shake it into your kvass and remove it from your milk kefir or sourdough starter. Mother cultures can be recultured and vegetables can be eaten, so you should rest assured that if everything else looks fine, your ferment does not need to go into the wastebasket.

Mold: When to Be Concerned

Now that you know that a white yeast is not necessarily a big deal, you are probably wondering how to know when you *should* be concerned. Here is a checklist you can run through if you ever have a question about a ferment:

1. **Smell it.** The best way to discern the health of any ferment is simply to smell it. It can smell sour, pungent, very fermented and even very yeasty. (I'm looking at you, milk kefir and sourdough!) But it should not smell putrid, rotten or incredibly disgusting. If it does not pass this test, throw it out and start over. If it does, move on to the next item. If you are a beginner and don't know what it should smell like, ask a friend or take the safest route possible.

2. **Check the color of the surface yeast.** Is it white? Then it's probably fine, but you can go ahead and do the smell test again. Is there any green, pink, yellow or blue? If so, I'd toss it. Even if it smells okay, this is a deal-breaker for me personally.

3. **Taste it.** If it smells strongly of tang or yeast, but does not smell rotten, and if it has no crazy colors to it, then it should be fine to taste it. This can be done for a kvass or a fermented vegetable. It might be extra tangy or yeasty, or it might taste just as a fermented beverage or vegetable should taste. In either case, it is fine to consume. If the taste is too strong, then you may want to add it to the compost pile anyway. If it is a mother culture like milk kefir grains or sourdough, scrape off the mold and reculture it in fresh milk or with another feeding of flour and water.

With practice, you will learn how to read signs of distress in your ferments. Until then, follow this guide and do what feels safe to you.

HOW TO EAT FERMENTED FOODS EVERY DAY

If you make fermented foods and you know how to turn them into something delicious, they will make it into your meals. So eating fermented foods every day, or even at every meal, is a foregone conclusion when you are working with them on a weekly basis to preserve and use the harvest to its fullest extent.

Perhaps you aren't using fermentation as a sustainability tool yet but you still want the benefits of fermented foods in your daily diet. We've been there. The simplest approach is to begin by making an array of fermented foods so you have options.

Keeping a cultured dairy, fermented vegetable and fermented beverage on hand at all times will ensure that you have probiotic, enzymatic choices.

The second step is to replace store-bought foods with the fermented foods you are making at home. With recipes for salad dressings, desserts, baked goods, main dishes and everything in between, my hope is that this book will assist you in this crucial step.

HOW TO USE THIS BOOK

The recipes in these pages were developed in my off-grid kitchen. As such, they are designed to work without refrigeration. I do, however, often provide instructions for refrigeration, knowing that many readers utilize it. Likewise, very conservative shelf-life estimates are given in the vegetable chapter (page 23); one or more years is not an uncommon shelf-life for these foods.

My passion for fermented foods extends way beyond recipes and formulas. While I hope the recipes in this book help and inspire you, they are not the end in and of themselves. The purpose of this book, from my point of view, is to help you create sustainable nourishment for you and your loved ones through fermentation.

This book is about sharing the many benefits and wonders of fermented foods for nourishment, for sustainability and for a way forward in departing from an industrialized food system. I truly believe that these foods are a very important piece in a very important puzzle.

May these recipes stand with you in the kitchen to preserve your plenty. May this book guide you toward using the provisions you have been given to their utmost. And may you nourish and be nourished by the work of your hands, the fruit of the land and traditionally fermented foods.

Vegetables

I don't know that I could have fully appreciated vegetable fermentation without first deeply understanding the joy and heartbreak of the agrarian pursuit. In the spring, there is a flurry of soil, seeds and hope on our homestead. To sow, water and wait is an act of faith; the results not always the stuff that January seed catalog dreams are made of; the process always just what we needed.

If we come to harvest and the bugs or rabbits have not pilfered, the water has been sufficient and the extremes in temperature have not oppressed, there are vegetables. And when you see that process through from start to an often painful finish, you know the true worth of what goes onto your plate.

And so we eat all that we can in that window of harvest. Plates heaped with barely steamed green beans, salads twice a day and potatoes that taste of the earth. Once we cannot take another bite, it is time to preserve what remains.

This is where I fell in love with fermented vegetables.

I wanted to retain as much nutritive value in those vegetables as the sweat equity I put into them demanded. I couldn't bring myself to boil them into mushy oblivion, their green vibrancy giving way to lackluster lifelessness. I wanted to preserve those vegetables and all that went into them, in a way that would, at the very least, allow them to retain their integrity. And I wanted it to be simple and require very little energy resources.

This brought me back to ancient practices and traditional techniques. Before refrigeration and freezing, before canning and jarring, before everything we ate was deadened by sterilization and pasteurization, there was lactic acid fermentation.

The Role of Fermentation in Food Preservation

I believe that fermenting, canning and dehydration all have a place as methods of food preservation. In fact, I often do all three when we have an abundance of something. Just as we like to diversify the types of trees and vegetables we grow in order to avoid putting all of our eggs in one basket, I see diversification as necessary in the putting up process. Canning is the brute force method of ensuring long-term food storage, and it has its place. Dehydration is a great method of food preservation in drier climates, and one I use most frequently—next to fermentation, of course. And of course, fermentation provides us with both short- and long-term food storage, and is the winner for enzymatic activity and nutrient density.

THE SCIENCE BEHIND LACTIC ACID FOOD PRESERVATION

It seems too good to be true, to think that covering vegetables in salt water not only keeps them from rotting, but also enhances things like vitamins, beneficial bacterial counts and enzymes. But it's true: You can make batches of any size in minutes and they will go about the work of preserving themselves while you get started on your other chores.

To understand how fermented vegetables are preserved, consider other means of food preservation. These techniques are all based on the knowledge that harmful bacteria cannot proliferate in an environment that is acidic, lacks moisture or lacks oxygen.

Dehydration works by removing moisture. The practice of larding or preserving in fat creates an oxygen-free environment for foods like duck confit to exist in. Vinegar pickling was once done without the extra step of water bath canning, knowing that the simple act of placing food in a liquid with sufficient acidity would prevent bacteria from taking hold.

Likewise, lactic acid fermentation creates an acidic, mostly anaerobic environment in which the vegetables are kept from undesirable bacteria such as the one that causes the dreaded botulism. This all begins in the soil, actually, as the microorganisms necessary for healthy soil are transferred to the vegetables it produces. (This is why I do not recommend peeling or heavily washing vegetables used for fermentation.) This beneficial bacteria, when placed in the proper environment, multiplies rapidly, producing various organic acids, yeasts, bacteria and gases.

It is the acids that are primarily responsible for the preservation, with lactic acid making up the greater part of the brine's acidity. Acetic acid—the acid found in vinegar—is also produced. This all happens in quick order once the vegetables are placed in the brine. In the earliest hours and days of fermentation, specific bacteria begin to drop the brine's pH. Once the brine is acidic enough, those bacteria pass the baton, in a way, to the bacteria that can exist only in an acidic environment, then these bacteria produce more acids and beneficial bacteria so that, all things being as they ought to, you have a living, bubbling, acidic fermented vegetable in a matter of days.

But the work is not over yet. You can eat fermented vegetables at this stage, but it is a myth that seeing carbonation means that the fermentation is complete. In fact, carbon dioxide is only given off in the earliest stages of fermentation by those bacteria that work to drop the pH. Once the brine is fairly acidic, the carbon dioxide production tapers off, which is why "burping" jars to release the pent-up gases is only necessary in the first week or two, depending on the temperature at which you ferment.

UNDERSTANDING WHY VEGETABLE FERMENTATION IS INHERENTLY SAFE

In my earliest days of vegetable fermentation, I was wary of feeding my family sauerkraut and pickles for fear that I would poison them. While I have come a long way, I have a feeling that I was not alone in this concern. I, for one, think that sometimes fear can be healthy.

What I didn't understand was that my fear of botulism was rooted in my understanding of water bath or pressure canned foods, not in the context of pickled or fermented foods. These are very different preservation techniques and a simple understanding of the contrast helped to put my mind at ease.

Canned foods that are acidic are canned using a water bath method. Fruits, tomatoes and vinegar pickles are all jarred, sealed and placed into a pot of boiling water for a specific period of time. These foods are preserved by a combination of their acidity, boiling out any bacteria and creating a vacuum seal within the jar.

Canned foods that are not acidic must be canned using a pressure canner. These jars are put under a great deal of pressure and heat, killing off any bacteria that might be present in the food. The vacuum seal ensures that no further bacterial contamination can take place.

Both of the above methods for canning foods use brute force to deaden the food and remove any and all bacteria present, even the beneficial ones.

Fermented vegetables, on the other hand, harness the natural bacteria present on the food to create an environment in which harmful bacteria cannot exist. As mentioned previously, the acids produced in short order through the fermentation process will not allow for the presence of the bacteria that causes botulism. In fact, the World Health Organization put out a publication about fermentation stating that, "From the food safety point of view, the benefits of fermentation include the inhibition of the growth of most pathogenic bacteria and the formation of bacterial toxins." (See http://www.who.int/foodsafety/publications/fs_management/fermentation.pdf).

That isn't to say that some batches of fermented vegetables won't go off. Sometimes you forget to thoroughly clean your equipment. Sometimes the vegetables themselves were a little beyond fresh. Sometimes produce, especially when purchased from large food systems, contains harmful bacteria due to poor farming practices. Whatever the case, you will be hard-pressed to consume a jar of sauerkraut that has not been properly fermented.

It is the living nature of fermented foods that preserves them and gives us a clear indication that they have not been safely preserved. Whereas a jar of canned green beans could be contaminated and have no unpleasant smell or distinguishing characteristic, a fermented food that has gone bad is clearly evident to the eye and the nose. Properly fermented vegetables have a very specific, pleasantly acidic smell. They also often smell of the type of vegetable themselves; for example, cruciferous vegetables such as cabbage give off a strong smell characteristic of their high sulfur content.

Therefore, all you need to do to determine the safety of a jar of fermented vegetables is to open it and hold it to your nose. I have done this with hundreds of jars and crocks of various vegetable ferments. Through smell I have immediately detected the dozen or fewer that have gone wrong in my decade of fermenting vegetables. Because of the living nature of fermented vegetables, there is also often a colorful mold on the surface of the brine of rotten ferments.

Anecdotally, of the hundreds of vegetable ferments my husband and I have consumed over the past ten years, neither of us has gotten sick once. In fact, when we get food poisoning from restaurant food or when some other type of bacterial digestive disorder goes through our home, consuming homemade raw fermented vegetables, milk kefir and kombucha seems to be the most helpful cure.

Best Practices for Safe and Delicious Ferments

The caveat, of course, is that you need to pay attention and go through the process of fermentation with a careful eye toward safety. Follow these tips for the safest, most delicious vegetable ferments.

Fresh is best. When I began to understand that the vegetables themselves were acting as a starter culture in the fermentation process, a lightbulb went on for me. The microorganisms present in the raw food are necessary for proper fermentation; therefore it is critical to ferment them in their purest, freshest state. That means trying to ferment them as soon after harvest as possible, as both the nutritional qualities and beneficial bacterial counts diminish with time. It also means you shouldn't peel your vegetables, because that is where the good bacteria are coming from.

Organic makes a difference. Likewise, you want to avoid anything that will impede the natural bacterial processes. Chemical pesticides, herbicides and fertilizers are all, by their very nature, antithetical to the natural process of bacterial fermentation. I have fermented all types of produce, from homegrown and organic to commercial and sprayed. In every single case, I have found that the vegetables closest to home, grown with absolutely zero unnatural interference, ferment swiftly and acidify rapidly. They also tend to have the best flavor and texture when eaten.

Keep it pure. Don't add anything that might impede the fermentation or acidification process. I generally don't like to add things like oils or animal foods to vegetable ferments that I would like to preserve for long-term storage. Historically and culturally, there are various accounts of preserving small amounts of meat in vegetable ferments with the goal of preserving the meat for short-term storage. For the sake of vegetable fermentation, keeping the ingredient list to salt, water and foods from the plant kingdom tends to allow the fermentation process to go off without a hitch.

Use clean equipment. I confess that I almost never sterilize anything in our home. For one, I don't subscribe to the common germ theory. I tend to think that bacteria, in most cases, is actually good, and that there is a reason that studies are finding that children in continual contact with dirt and animals tend to have fewer health problems than those who are not. Secondly, I just don't find it necessary. A good washing in soapy water tends to do the trick. That said, I do like to examine my bowls and cutting boards for cleanliness and make sure that the jars into which I'll be packing the ferments have been washed well so as to avoid any competing bacteria in the jar.

Water quality is important. Besides the vegetables and salt, clean water is really the only other ingredient you need to think about. Any type of chemical-free water is fine but unless you have a well or you catch rainwater as we do, there is often no telling what might be in your water. For that reason, getting a high-quality water filter is helpful no matter where you live. If you do not own a filter, one popular method for reducing the chlorine in city water is to leave it out, uncovered overnight. This supposedly helps to off-gas the chlorine from the water.

Submersion is key. Always, *always* make every effort to keep your vegetables submerged under the brine. This is how vegetables ferment and are therefore preserved, so if there are any rules to vegetable fermentation, this is one of them. Things like radishes often poke their little heads up above the brine, as do cabbage shreds or herbs. These things happen and most of the time they do not negatively impact the ferment batch on the whole, passing the sniff test with flying colors. That said, making every effort to weight the vegetables down so that they stay below the surface of the brine tends to ensure better flavor, longer shelf life and less surface yeast.

BRINE LEVEL AND PROPER BURPING: THE KEYS TO AN ANAEROBIC MASON JAR FERMENT

To drive home just how important keeping your vegetables below the level of the brine is, I'd like to paint a picture for you. Picture a quart (1-L)-size jar filled with vegetables up to the three-cup (710-ml) mark. Now picture brine rising to the bottom of the part of the jar where the ring is screwed on. That gives you a full inch (25 mm) of brine above the ferment.

In this scenario, the vegetables are separated from oxygen by three layers. The brine keeps them in an anaerobic state. The carbon dioxide in the jar, between the brine and lid, displaces the oxygen. The lid then keeps all of these elements separated from the oxygen outside the jar.

For this reason, I recommend packing the jars approximately 80 percent full. Use extra brine to allow for a maximum of one inch (25 mm) of headspace. This extra brine insures that the anaerobic environment is maintained, even if the carbon dioxide escapes entirely and allows oxygen in, but it also adds another piece of insurance. With the level of the vegetables further beneath the surface of the brine, you can remove any surface yeast soon after formation without disturbing the vegetables themselves.

The other critical piece of this equation is the proper "burping" technique. You want some carbon dioxide to remain in the jar. So when you burp the jar, do a very quick twist, allow some of the gas to release and then tighten the jar back up. The lid should not give too much when pressed on. Because you are not releasing much of the gas, the jars need to be checked and burped frequently in the first three to five days of fermentation. After that, carbon dioxide production tapers off and the pH of the fermented vegetables has dropped quite a bit, making it more difficult for yeasts and molds to take hold.

THE RELATIONSHIP BETWEEN SALT, TEMPERATURE AND TIME

If you want to learn to ferment any vegetable under any conditions, then it is helpful to understand the symbiosis of salt, temperature and time in the fermentation process. The speed at which the fermentation process takes place can affect the final flavor and shelf life of the vegetable. Generally speaking, a slower fermentation process creates optimal flavor and shelf life.

The bacterial activity affects the flavor of a fermented vegetable. Bacteria specific to sauerkraut and cucumber pickles have been identified. These bacteria contribute to the flavor of the fermented vegetable. The bacterial activity is affected by the rate at which it ferments. Generally speaking, a slower fermentation process allows for the full range of bacteria to play out in a natural way, which results in better flavor. A slower fermentation is also a cooler fermentation, and cooler temperatures help the vegetable fibers remain intact, which results in a crisper ferment.

Salt plays a pretty critical role in both the taste of the final ferment and the time it takes to ferment the vegetable. Salt helps to maintain the structural integrity of the vegetable fiber, which is a fancy way of saying that it helps it maintain the crunch. Salt also slows down the fermentation process so that under warmer conditions, fermentation does not happen so rapidly as to lose the integrity of the flavor and texture of the vegetable. Fermented vegetables are not preserved by salt, per se, in the way that salt pork is. Rather, salt is a catalyst for optimal fermentation—slowing it down to just the right pace, allowing the vegetable to stand up to the process. Salt can be omitted, but not without a compromise in flavor, texture and shelf life.

You will notice that many recipe authors call for a range of salt, depending on the temperature at which you are fermenting. *Salt slows fermentation down while an increase in temperature speeds it up.* You can therefore optimize the fermentation time by increasing or decreasing the salt content. If you will be fermenting in a very cool environment (50 to 70°F [10 to 21°C]), 2 tablespoons (30 g) of salt per quart (946 ml) of vegetables should be sufficient. If you are fermenting in a warmer environment (70 to 90°F [21 to 32°C]), 3 tablespoons (45 g) of salt will help slow the process down without creating an overly salty ferment.

The temperature at which you ferment vegetables can have a huge impact on how they taste and how long they keep. Warmer temperatures will speed up the rate at which the fermentative bacteria work on the vegetables. This can result in a breakdown of the vegetable cellulose, giving you mushy vegetables and yeasty, off flavors. I have also found that undesirable yeasts and molds form more readily in the summer months.

The bottom line is that a slower fermentation over a longer period of time is generally going to result in a better end product. Slowing down fermentation through the manipulation of temperature and salt is therefore the name of the game.

On a personal note, I live in a pretty hot climate where the months of June through September can easily be 90 to 100°F (32 to 38°C) every single day. Knowing that, and given the fact that our gardens are actually least productive during this period due to both the heat and the lack of rain, I usually ferment for short-term storage in the summer and for long-term storage in the fall. This is just another way in which vegetable fermentation can be personalized to your needs and environment.

KNOWING WHEN YOUR FERMENT IS DONE

It is a myth that seeing your fermented vegetable bubbling means that it is through with the fermentation process. This actually is an indication that the fermentation is in its earliest stages, as carbon dioxide is generally produced by those bacteria that cannot exist in a more acidic environment. As the pH drops, carbon dioxide production slows down and other bacteria take over the fermentation process. The proliferation of these bacteria create flavors, textures and bacterial counts available only in fermented foods that have been allowed to run their natural course.

There is a sweet spot, however. I'm not sure how many hundreds of jars of ferments we've made and consumed, but it is that experience, and no scientific paper I am aware of, that indicates that fermented foods in general have a window within the fermentation process at which they are most alive. This is when not only the beneficial bacterial counts are highest, but the enzyme action in the ferment is at its peak. It also happens to coincide with the time when the flavor has developed but is not overly acidic. In other words, it is the ideal time to eat the vegetable ferment for both flavor and health reasons.

It is impossible to tell you exactly when a vegetable ferment has hit this sweet spot. Even in a 70 to 80°F (21 to 27°C) environment, I generally find that most vegetables are best after two to three weeks at warm room temperature. At cooler temperatures, or if you move your ferments to cold storage, you could be looking at one to three months or more. Remember that the process of fermentation does not stop simply because you move it into cold storage. Unless cold storage is very cold, the process continues but at a much slower pace.

Beyond giving your ferments at least a couple of weeks at room temperature, your taste buds should be your guide. Once you make enough fermented vegetables, you should be able to identify the stages of fermentation. Early on, ferments tend to be very bright and salad-like; the vegetable fibers are still nearly as firm as the raw vegetable and the acids are not fully developed. After this phase, you get into that sweet spot where the whole pickle is tangy, but not puckeringly so. The texture is still crunchy but not like a raw vegetable. It has gained maturity from the weeks or months of aging but has not gotten so acidic that it has lost some of its vitality. That is the sweet spot.

Another good sign is if your ferments are well out of the "burp" zone. During that first five to seven days, you will need to check the jars frequently for built-up pressure. Once the carbon dioxide production tapers off, it is a good idea to give the ferment at least two to three more weeks to ripen before you move it to cold storage.

THE WHEN AND HOW OF COLD STORAGE

The Impact of Storage Temperature on Your Ferments

In my experience, the ideal temperature range for fermentation is 55 to 75°F (13 to 24°C). The higher end of that spectrum will result in more rapid fermentation. The ideal storage temperature is 40 to 60°F (4 to 16°C). When a ferment is moved to cold storage in a 35°F (2°C) refrigerator, the fermentation can come to a screeching halt. The fermentation process will drastically slow down at 40 to 50°F (4 to 10°C), allowing it to continue (thereby preserving the vegetable) for months. You can also store the ferment right at room temperature, just expect a tangier flavor with a shortened shelf life.

You have a few options when it comes to how and where you ferment your vegetables. You can ferment them at room temperature for a longer period of time and then move them to a very cold environment (35 to 45°F [2 to 7°C]) to drastically slow down the fermentation. You can ferment them for a few weeks at room temperature and then move them to a moderately cool storage place (45 to 60°F [7 to 16°C]).

If your coolest storage space is above 60°F (16°C), you may want to simply commence with fermentation right in the storage space. Keep in mind that you will still need to burp the jars regularly, which may be a bit inconvenient. I suspect that when our pioneering ancestors made crocks of kraut and pickles, the jars went straight to the cellar for a very long, very slow fermentation period. This may have happened during a time of the year when the cellar was warmer. As fall approached, the cellar slowly cooled day by day, thereby creating a natural tapering into cold storage for the winter months.

Once your vegetables have fermented at room temperature for a couple of weeks, it is important to decide whether you plan to keep the fermented vegetables in long-term storage (three to six months or more) or short-term storage (one to three months). The latter can be done at room temperature if your average daytime temperature is at or below 80°F (27°C). If it is warmer than that, and if you want to store your vegetables for a longer period of time, you should move them to a colder environment.

COLD STORAGE WITHOUT REFRIGERATION

The very first ferments I made were a terrible way to introduce fermented vegetables to my family. They tasted like really salty cabbage with just a hint of tang. It took a long time for my husband to agree to try another batch.

And then I met a Ukrainian woman who had grown up with sauerkraut. "Too much salt!" she said—and too soon. So I cut way back on the salt and let it sit out twice as long before refrigerating. Better, but still not great. So I left the jars in the fridge for literally seven months. We ate salsa in February from last July's tomatoes and it was perfectly preserved and tasted much better than those feeble first attempts.

Fast-forward a few years and we moved off-grid. A small solar freezer/refrigerator and occasional coolers were our new cold storage norm and they were stocked with foods like cheese and fresh meat that weren't meant to preserve themselves. Knowing that fermented foods preserve themselves and knowing that I really didn't have any other options, I began testing my preconceived limits with fermented vegetable storage.

After about a year, I realized that the ferments that were stored at cool or warm room temperature almost always tasted better than the refrigerated counterparts. The flavors were well developed, the balance of tang, spice and fresh were all perfectly melded. I then realized the only difference was that these ferments had never seen a refrigerator.

The purpose of moving ferments to cold storage is to slow down the fermentation process. Remember that the warmer the temperature, the faster the fermentation rate. So once the fermentation process is well underway, you'll want to find a *cooler* place to store the ferments for longer shelf life. Of course, if you are using fermentation as a means of short-term storage, as we often do, then no cold storage is required. If you want your ferments to last for months, however, then slowing down the fermentation process is important.

Refrigeration is an option but keep in mind that the bacteria cycled through during the fermentation process have specific needs both in temperature and pH. There are some bacteria that can only proliferate below certain temperatures and others that can only proliferate above certain temperatures. A refrigerator is meant to keep food between 32°F (0°F) and 40°F (4°C). It is at 40°F (4°C) when experts say the "danger zone" begins. This danger zone in which bacteria proliferate the fastest is from 40 to 140°F (4 to 60°C).

So when we put a jar of sauerkraut that is at some stage in the fermentation process into the refrigerator, we are putting it into an environment that is *designed to prevent* the proliferation of bacteria. Prevention of bacteria is good, if you don't want your hamburger to rot on the counter. It is not so good if you are trying to encourage the proliferation of *good* bacteria in an anaerobic environment specifically geared toward their growth. This doesn't mean that refrigeration can't be used to store your fermented vegetables, it just means that there is a difference in the final product between refrigerated ferments and those stored in a slightly warmer environment. Sometimes five to ten degrees can make all the difference.

It has been five years now since I've used any type of refrigeration to store my fermented vegetables. In that time, we've come to love kraut and pickles even more. I put this down to the fact that they are now a huge part of the sustainable food system we are trying to create in our home kitchen. More than that, we all agree that they taste much better. The longer fermentation time coupled with the lack of refrigeration creates a balance and complexity in flavor that we simply were not getting previously.

While refrigeration can be used and certainly won't harm your fermented vegetables, you might be looking for alternative cold storage methods to keep your ferments longer. Here are a few ideas:

Root cellar or basement. This is the most obvious choice, especially if you live in a cooler climate. These locations can often have an optimal ferment storage temperature of 45 to 60°F (7 to 16°C), which will aid in keeping your ferments for months.

A simple hole. I know this sounds archaic, but a simple hole in the ground mimics a full-blown root cellar quite nicely. You can place a box or cooler inside the hole for protection from dirt or you can place a sealed crock or jar directly into the ground. You can then cover it with a board or other covering to keep animals out. You can also simply bury the vessels in dirt. Again, this seems quite extreme to our Western minds, but it is a common practice in traditional cultures. Burying the sealed vessels also keeps out oxygen, which is a boon to the anaerobic fermentation process.

An unheated room. Often times there are spaces in our homes that are cooler. These are the unheated rooms in the colder months, or the sides of the house less exposed to the warmth of the sun. You can place a thermometer in various areas of your home to detect the most ideal place for fermented vegetable storage.

HOW TO AVOID MUSHY FERMENTS

Besides going bad, one of the worst fates a fermented pickle can meet is to go to mush. It's a shame because they are quite unpleasant to eat and this is easily avoidable. If you do have a run-in with mushy vegetables, don't just toss them out! Make something akin to an Overfermented Salsa Hot Sauce (page 206), which is a delicious way to serve less-than-crunchy ferments.

To avoid mushy ferments, I recommend the following guidelines:

Use fresh vegetables. As soon as you pick a vegetable or fruit, the nutritional and structural integrity starts heading down a slow path toward decay. It therefore stands to reason that fresher vegetables maintain their structural integrity better than those that have traveled across continents or have sat on the counter for days or weeks.

Ferment at cooler temperatures. This isn't always possible, and the tannins mentioned below help, but when possible, choose a cooler location in which your vegetables can ferment. Anything above 85°F (29°C) tends to break down the cellulose (vegetable fiber) in the ferment, causing it to go to mush much more easily.

Use enough salt. In order to counteract concerns over temperature and also to help the vegetable fibers generally maintain their integrity, salt is crucial. Ferments easily become mushy when salt is omitted or skimped on.

Add tannin-containing leaves to your ferments. Besides salt, tannins are helpful in maintaining the structural integrity of the vegetable fibers. In fact, this one simple addition can revolutionize your pickle making. This can be as organic as heading out to your yard or nearby forest and picking a handful of grape, oak, horseradish or mesquite leaves. If these are not available, the common tea plant (think black tea) contains a good deal of tannins. A small pinch of the loose tea leaves in a ferment will keep your vegetables crunchy while going completely unnoticed.

Cut off the blossom end of your vegetable. Even old pickle recipes that call for a strong vinegar brine often recommend that you remove the ends of your vegetables. This is due to an enzyme produced in the blossom end of the vegetable that can work to soften the vegetable. Trimming both ends of cucumbers, squash and other vegetables should do the trick.

ON STARTER CULTURES

A starter culture is an ingredient in a fermented vegetable recipe that is added to kick-start the process with a bit of bacteria. Some say these cultures are absolutely necessary for good ferments, while others don't like to use them at all. I have been on both sides of the fence, falling further within the latter category as time went on.

A few of the starter cultures often called for in vegetable fermentation recipes include:

1. Whey strained from cultured dairy products

2. Brine from a previous batch of fermented vegetables

3. Kombucha or water kefir

4. Culture starter powder from a proprietary blend of microorganisms.

5. Raw apple cider vinegar

Before I tell you why I don't use these anymore, let me tell you why I did when I first got started. I added whey to my earliest batches of sauerkraut and pickles. Because I was not familiar with the process, the idea that my vegetable ferments would start out with a dose of bacteria put my mind at ease. And I actually think this is a great first step for those trying to get started with fermentation.

I stopped adding starter cultures to my vegetable ferments when I began to understand how vegetable fermentation works on a biological level. There is a process happening that starts when you place vegetables containing trace amounts of bacteria into an anaerobic environment. These bacteria multiply naturally to lower the pH, create enzymes and preserve the food through lactic acid bacteria proliferation and lactic acid production. Any introduction of microorganisms will compete with the natural process.

So you certainly can use a starter culture, but be aware that by inoculating the ferment with the microorganisms in whey or even brine from a previous batch of fermented vegetables, you are encouraging *those* bacteria to proliferate. And as I mentioned earlier, there is a baton that passes from one set of bacteria to the next naturally as the pH drops and the bacteria proliferate.

Therefore, adding a culture starter can change the final flavor, texture and bacterial profile. This isn't necessarily a bad thing, and some fermenters only make vegetable ferments with culture starters. All of that said, I personally do not find it necessary and, all other elements being equal, prefer the flavor of fermented vegetables that are allowed to go through the lactic acid fermentation process naturally.

The one thing I would discourage is adding vinegar, and even kombucha, as a starter culture. Acetic acid—the acid found in vinegar—is actually produced in small amounts during the fermentation process. It competes, however, with a great deal of lactic acid, and lactic acid is the one we want to encourage during fermentation. It is therefore contrary to the natural fermentation process we are trying to encourage to add acetic acid-containing starter cultures such as vinegar or kombucha.

The bottom line is that if you are making every effort to use the right ingredients, equipment and techniques outlined above, there is absolutely no need for a starter culture. Furthermore, starter cultures can actually inhibit the natural process we are attempting to encourage.

Fermented Vegetable Brine, the Unsung Hero

When you make brine-fermented vegetables like Kosher Dill Pickles (page 51) or Everyday Spicy Carrots (page 56), you end up with not one but two edible, probiotic-rich products. In fact, I would argue that the one we consume isn't even the most valuable. Fermented vegetable brine is liquid gold in our house. It is not unlike a kvass in that it is teeming with enzymes and probiotics, but with added salt to give it an added electrolytic punch. See the recipe for Vegetable Brine Wellness Shots on page 186 for one way to drink it.

EQUIPMENT

Of Jars, Crocks and Airlocks

Somehow we have ended up with staunch camps in the debate over fermentation equipment, as if the common polarized rhetoric of the day had a place here. You don't have to look too far into the historical and cultural practices of vegetable fermentation to find out that there are no hard and fast rules.

In Korea, crocks of kimchi are prepared, sealed with a crockery lid and then buried for months on end. In the South Pacific, pits are dug and vegetables are fermented and then buried right in the dirt. In Northern Europe, large crocks of kraut and pickles are weighted down in Grandma's cellar, and the unpleasant foam or yeast is scraped from the surface when a portion is removed from the crock. In my own kitchen, and in many others in North America, we like to use glass mason jars.

All of these methods work if employed properly, and you'd be hard-pressed to argue with the practices of these ancient cultures that had no airlocks or quart jars. In other words, use what you have. The equipment used in vegetable fermentation needs to be watertight, spacious enough for your chosen batch size, with a wide enough mouth to slip a weight in there, and covered with a lid (permeable or solid) in order to keep bugs out. Also keep in mind that fermented vegetables are acidic, which means you will want to avoid metal.

Common fermentation equipment includes:

Glass jars and lids. These are readily available in most kitchens. I personally employ jars of pint (0.5 L), quart (1 L), half-gallon (2 L) and gallon (4 L) sizes for vegetable fermentation. The lids and rings that come with these (or the solid metal lid that comes with the gallon size) work fine for fermentation.

What Size Jars Should I Ferment In?

If you do not have cold storage and you are using glass jars, choose a size that will feed your family within three to four meals. When storing fermented vegetables on the counter in glass canning jars with lids and rings, I find that the surface starts to accumulate yeast much faster once it has been opened (after the initial fermentation-burping period). To avoid this, I break up a gallon (4 L) jar of sauerkraut into four quart (1-L)-size jars for our larger family, knowing we will consume the contents of that jar within three meals and that the remaining three quarts will remain unopened until needed. Pint (0.5-L)-size jars may work well for smaller families.

Airlocks. These are similar to the carboys you see used for homebrewing. Essentially, they allow the carbon dioxide produced through the vegetable fermentation process to escape while not allowing air to be introduced. Many people feel that airlocks are necessary to avoid mold and maximize the lactic acid bacteria counts of your fermented vegetables. If you have a health condition that makes you sensitive to histamines or wild (beneficial) yeasts, this may be a good option for you. Otherwise, besides the convenience of not having to burp your jars, airlocks are not necessary for successful fermentation. I personally rarely use them.

Crocks. These too come in a variety of sizes that can be employed for long- or short-term storage. There are crocks with lids that seal using a sort of mote of water at the top of the crock. Although expensive, they are a valuable investment since they can be used for years to come. Crocks without lids are also available. You pack the vegetables into the crock and often place a plate and other weight to keep the vegetables below the brine. A clean towel or a tight-weave cheesecloth are then needed to keep out fruit flies and unwanted debris. These are great for long-term storage for those who have a basement or cellar that maintains a cool 40 to 60°F (4 to 16°C) during storage.

Fermentation Weights

Besides choosing a decent vessel and fresh ingredients, nothing could be more critical to the quality of your fermented vegetables than weighing down the vegetables so they remain under the brine. The lactic acid fermentation process is an anaerobic one, meaning the bacteria involved need an environment lacking in oxygen in order to work properly. The salt brine used to ferment vegetables is just the ticket as long as those vegetables stay below the level of the brine. The vegetables' buoyancy and escaping gases can cause them to float to the surface. Fermentation weights, and plenty of them, help to keep those vegetables down.

If you are using a crock, a large heavy plate topped with other clean, heavy kitchen items can work. Just be sure to get everything covered tightly with a clean tea towel or tightly woven cheesecloth to keep unwanted bugs and debris out.

If you are fermenting with jars, there are several options available:

Fermentation weights. You can purchase ceramic and glass disks for use as fermentation weights. If I were to purchase a piece of equipment, this would probably be my first investment. These are really handy to plunk into the jar before sealing, though I find that I generally have to use more than one to really keep the vegetables down. I have also seen small stainless steel cups that you fill with water to weight down the vegetables. I personally do not use these as I try to avoid direct contact between the acidic fermented vegetables and all types of metal.

Cabbage leaves and cores. One common way to hold down kraut is with the tough outer leaves of the cabbage. These are thick and sturdy, and can be manipulated to fit right into the jar. Push them down atop your vegetables and allow brine to pool over the concave leaf, adding a bit more weight. The cores are also nice and dense and, when cut to fit the jar opening, make a great addition.

Root vegetable plugs. Thick slices of beet, turnip, daikon radish and even large carrots can be used as weights. These should be cut to fit the size of the jar opening and be at least ½ inch (13 mm) thick to be heavy enough to do the job. Using these in conjunction with the cabbage leaves works well.

Apple slices. Cut thick slices of fresh apple and then create a doughnut hole in the middle using a vegetable peeler. The sugars in the apple will add a bit of extra flavor to whatever you ferment.

Nested jam jars. Smaller jars can fit into the opening of quart (1-L)- or half-gallon (2-L)-size jars. These should be clean, and you will need to fasten a clean cloth around the jar to keep unwanted bugs and debris out of your ferment.

Whichever option you choose, keep in mind that you need something *heavy* to truly keep those vegetables weighted down. Sometimes this means employing more than one of the options listed here.

USING FERMENTED VEGETABLES

I have always thought that the benefits of fermented vegetables are only as good as the amounts you are willing and able to eat. In other words, make tasty ferments and serve them in unique ways. Anything else is a waste of your time and resources.

With that in mind, here are some tips for eating fermented vegetables every single day. Start with tasty recipes and then incorporate them into just about anything.

Fourteen Ways to Eat Fermented Vegetables

When I make a big batch of fermented vegetables, I think of it as the ultimate convenience food. It's a stand-in for salads, nutritionally speaking, and turns any one-pot meal into a well-balanced feast. In case you need a little more inspiration, here are some of the many ways we like to eat krauts and pickles of all kinds:

1. Next to eggs, grains, beans, roasted vegetables or meat.

2. Mixed into avocado, sour cream or cream cheese for use as a delicious spread.

3. Tossed into fresh green salads, mixing the brine with olive oil as a vinaigrette.

4. Atop pizza that has cooled enough to preserve the enzymes of the ferment.

5. Blended into smoothies at the rate of ¼ to ½ cup (59 to 118 ml) per four servings.

6. Tossed with cooled pasta and fresh vegetables for a picnic salad.

7. Mixed into your favorite tuna, chicken or ham salad for sandwiches.

8. Added to breakfast, meat or bean tacos.

9. Served alongside sandwiches in a lunchbox.

10. Added to a platter of cheese, charcuterie and fresh crudité.

11. Mixed into smashed beans for a vegetable dip or spread.

12. As part of a baked potato bar.

13. In place of slaw when serving a plate of barbecue.

14. Atop your favorite fresh sausages or burgers.

ABOUT THE RECIPES

I do a lot of fermenting simply using whatever ingredients I have on hand. Herbs go in when they need to be preserved alongside the vegetables. Garlic makes its way in for flavor and health. Random vegetable combinations come together when we have an abundance of produce to put up. That is the purely functional version of sustainable vegetable fermentation, and we eat these ferments with gusto.

Before our entire family got to the point of incorporating and loving all fermented vegetables, however, I worked at making ferments delicious. What is the point, after all, if no one will eat the many jars you've fermented when putting up the harvest? The right amount of salt, the right fermentation time and bold flavor are all a part of incorporating fermented vegetables easily into every meal.

The recipes you'll find in this chapter are just that—ferments with flavor and seasoning, crafted from seasonal ingredients and a desire for pure, tangy deliciousness. We're not just trying to hold our noses and shove down some probiotics here; we are going back for seconds and thirds from the ferment jar; we are hearing "Yes, kimchi!" when everyone gathers around the table.

One thing you'll notice is that I include ranges for items like fermentation time, storage time and salt quantities. The truth is, there is no way to know exactly how long it will take to ferment, how long the food will keep and how much salt is required due to the many variables that affect the fermentation process. Read through the section The Relationship Between Salt, Temperature and Time on page 27 for a better understanding of when to use the smaller amount of salt and when the larger might be necessary. Remember that fermentation time is sped up when it is warm, so it may not take quite as long to move through the process.

Finally, remember that storage time depends not only on the environment the jars are stored in but also the elements surrounding the initial fermentation, the state of your equipment and the produce your process began with. With all of that taken into account, the longer storage time reflects ideal conditions, but you should check the jars in long-term storage from time to time to see what needs to get eaten when.

Brined Vegetables vs. Self-Brining Ones

Once you have played with the vegetable ferment recipes in this chapter, I encourage you to experiment and be open-minded. To guide you along the way, I have included recipes for the two basic types of fermented vegetables—brined and self-brining.

Self-brining vegetables are those that are shredded, salted and pounded—or simply given time—to create their own brine. Sometimes additional brine is needed to top up the vegetables, especially if they are less than fresh, but for the most part, these vegetables make their own brine.

Brined vegetables are those that are left whole or cut into large chunks. These include dill pickles and fermented carrots or green beans. They make great snacks or can be chopped up to add to salads, dips or relishes.

Mason Jar Fermentation

All of the recipes are written using the most common fermentation vessel—the mason jar. The recipes generally make 1 to 2 quarts (946 to 1,892 ml), which can then be broken up into pint (0.5 L) jars for smaller families to keep jars sealed as long as possible.

There are now many gadgets that can be attached to mason jars to act as airlocks. They can be used on any ferment recipe; the only change to the directions is that you no longer have to burp the jar. There is an argument to be made that an airlock means you do not need to weigh your vegetables down and keep them below the level of the brine due to the anaerobic environment it creates. However, I feel that it is better to have weighed down your vegetables *and* airlocked than to have never weighed down your vegetables at all.

The Use and Diversity of These Recipes

When potatoes and beans are all you have, ferments lend enzymes and loads of flavor. When you are eating an abundance of stews, and greens are but a dream in the dead of winter, ferments fill the gap. When all you have time for is fried eggs and rice because there are seeds to plant in spring, ferments are the convenience food that makes it a meal.

I have attempted to give a wide variety of recipes so we can all take what grows well in our area and preserve it by lactic acid fermentation. I also included two recipes at the end in which ferments play a major role in a compiled dish.

My goal is to show the versatility and simplicity of lactic acid fermentation. There is no need to can the life out of all of your produce. Nor is there a need to hold your nose and throw ferments down the hatch. They can be simple to make and crazy delicious; they are convenience foods that also happen to be teeming with nourishment.

Fermented vegetables, in many ways, changed my life and the trajectory of our health and food-preservation practices. I hope these recipes do much the same for you and your loved ones.

Homestead 'Chi

Kimchi, when made right, is an easy crowd-pleaser. This is by far one of my favorite vegetable ferments for several reasons. The flavor is great, the ingredients are commonly found and the turnips that grow so easily but are eaten so begrudgingly are converted into a form our whole family loves.

 Makes: 2 quarts (1.9 kg) / Fermentation Time: At least 3 weeks / Storage Time: 6 to 12 months

2 medium heads green cabbage

2 large (softball-size) turnips, grated

12 green onions, chopped roughly

8 large garlic cloves, minced

3–4 tbsp (45–60 g) salt (4 tbsp [60 g] only if temperatures exceed 80°F [27°C])

3 tbsp (22 g) ground sweet paprika

1–2 tbsp (2–4 g) red pepper flakes or ¼–½ cup (43–85 g) diced hot peppers

Shred the cabbage thinly using a knife and cutting board or a mandolin. Add the cabbage and all remaining ingredients to a large mixing bowl. Mix well with hands to combine. Pound the cabbage with a mallet or potato masher to release the juices. Alternatively, allow to sit, covered, for 1 hour to allow the juices to be released.

Pack kimchi tightly into a half-gallon (2-L)-size jar or 2 quart (1-L)-size jars, leaving at least 2 inches (50 mm) of headspace. Add the fermentation weight of your choosing (page 33). Check that the brine is above the level of the fermentation weight. If not, mix 1 cup (236 ml) of water with 1½ teaspoons (8 g) of salt and pour this brine into the jar until the fermentation weight is completely covered.

Place at cool room temperature (60 to 80°F [16 to 27°C], optimally) and allow to ferment for at least three weeks. If you haven't used an airlock, then during this period, especially during the first 5 to 7 days, you will need to burp the jars by quickly opening them to release the built-up gases that result from the fermentation. To do so, carefully and quickly open the jar, listen for the release of gas and close the jar back up with just a bit of the gases still remaining inside.

This ferment pairs wonderfully with eggs, beans and salads, and makes a delicious spread when mixed with a soft cheese.

Summer Squash Cortido

There are a few vegetables that always seem to do well in our garden—turnips, black-eyed peas and summer squash, for instance. I like planting heirloom varieties like the Tatume squash from Mexico or the fast-growing Desi squash that produces abundant baseball-size fruit. Fermenting squash spears and rounds has long been a part of my summer food preservation, but this flavorful ferment that eats like a relish was a game-changer. The flavor profile is borrowed from the Latin American sauerkraut that we love, making it my new favorite way to ferment that morning squash harvest I carried in with my apron.

 Makes: 1 quart (946 ml) / Fermentation Time: 2 weeks / Storage Time: 2 to 4 months

4 cups (1.3 kg) packed, shredded summer squash or zucchini

1 medium carrot

2 garlic cloves

1½ tbsp (23 g) sea salt

2 tsp (1 g) dried oregano

¼–½ tsp red pepper flakes, as desired

Remove stem and blossom ends from the squash. Grate the squash into a medium-size mixing bowl using the largest holes of a box grater. Repeat with the carrot and then grate garlic into the bowl using the smallest holes of a box grater.

Add the salt, oregano and red pepper flakes and mix together well with clean hands or a wooden spoon. Allow to sit for at least 15 to 20 minutes to allow the salt to draw the brine from the squash.

Pack the vegetables into a clean quart (1-L)-size jar up to the 3 to 3½ cup (709 to 828 ml) mark. Weight down with the fermentation weight of your choosing (page 33) and seal the jar tightly.

Place at cool room temperature (60 to 80°F [16 to 27°C], optimally) and allow to ferment for at least two weeks. If you haven't used an airlock, then during this period, especially during the first 5 to 7 days, you will need to burp the jars by quickly opening them to release the built-up gases that result from fermentation. To do so, carefully and quickly open the jar, listen for the release of gas, and close the jar back up with just a bit of the gases still remaining inside.

The traditional cortido made with cabbage is served alongside pupusas. This cortido, likewise, is delicious with beans, meats, corn tortillas and all manner of south-of-the-border cuisine. It also makes a killer sandwich relish or baked potato topping.

Taco Kraut

Late spring often brings rain, warmer temperatures and cilantro. In our warmer climate, the cilantro plant is known to self-seed, bringing us little patches between the fava beans or near the freshly planted greens. Unhappily, this does not coincide with a tomato or tomatillo harvest. Instead, I pair it with cabbage in this ferment, preserving this delicious herb for as long as the kraut will last in our house. Which is to say, not all that long.

Makes: 2 quarts (1.9 L) / Fermentation Time: At least 3 weeks / Storage Time: 6 to 12 months

2 medium heads cabbage, shredded finely

2 cups (80 g) packed, rough-chopped cilantro

3 tbsp (45 g) sea salt

8 green onions, diced

2 jalapeños, seeded and chopped

6 large garlic cloves, minced

Combine all ingredients in a large bowl. Mix well with hands to combine. Pound the cabbage with a mallet or potato masher to release the juices. Alternatively, allow to sit, covered, for 1 hour to allow the juices to be released.

Pack kraut tightly into 1 half-gallon (2-L)-size jar or 2 quart (1-L)-size jars, leaving at least 2 inches (50 mm) of headspace. Add the fermentation weight of your choosing (page 33). Check that the brine is above the level of the fermentation weight. If not, mix 1 cup (237 ml) of water with 1½ teaspoons (8 g) of salt and pour this brine into the jar until the fermentation weight is completely covered.

Place at cool room temperature (60 to 80°F [16 to 27°C], optimally) and allow to ferment for at least 3 weeks. If you haven't used an airlock, then during this period, especially during the first 5 to 7 days, you will need to burp the jars by quickly opening them to release the built-up gases that result from fermentation. To do so, carefully and quickly open the jar, listen for the release of gas and close the jar back up with just a bit of the gases still remaining inside.

After 3 weeks, move to cold storage. This ferment is great on tacos of all kinds but also works well with beans, salads and quesadillas and alongside stir-fries.

Fermented Fresh Herbs

While dehydrating woody herbs such as oregano, thyme and rosemary really locks in the flavor, I find annual
herbs preserved by this method underwhelming. To remedy that, and because I can no longer freeze them,
I've come to love fermenting them in a brine or in a paste—their fresh flavor really comes through
with the introduction of lactic acid during fermentation.

It's a good idea to make small jars of these guys because you will only use a few leaves or a spoonful or two at a time.

 Makes: 8 ounces (237 ml) / Fermentation Time: 5 to 10 days, depending on temperature /
Storage Time: 3 to 6 months

BRINE-FERMENTED

1 cup (40 g) lightly packed, fresh, whole
herb leaves (any herb works here)

1 cup (237 ml) water

1 tsp (5 g) sea salt

CHOPPED/PASTE

2-3 bunches cilantro, parsley or basil

½ tsp fine-grain sea salt

VARIATIONS: While single herbs
are a great choice for picking and
choosing what you use them with,
mixed herbs create an all-seasons
approach. This herb mixture will
flavor everything from soups to
casseroles, sandwiches to spreads.
Just mix several of your favorite
herbs and add some onion or
garlic scapes for additional
flavoring. Use this in place of
the herb ration in the recipes
above. And don't forget that the
brine will make for an incredible
addition to vinaigrettes or Veg
Brine Mayonnaise (page 205).

For the Brine-Fermented Fresh Herbs, pack a 1-cup (237-ml) jam jar with the herb
leaves, leaving a bit of headspace. Combine the water and sea salt and pour over the
herbs. Weigh down as you would sauerkraut, cover and allow to ferment for 5 to
10 days or until tangy and bubbling.

Transfer to cold storage. Keeps for several months at room temperature if left unopened.
Will keep for 1 to 2 weeks at room temperature once opened or store for up to 6 months
when refrigerated.

The Chopped/Paste method turns out a roughly chopped paste that creates its own
brine, much like sauerkraut does.

Remove the cilantro leaves from the stems and chop them finely. Transfer to a small
bowl and toss with sea salt.

Transfer herbs, salt and any brine in the bottom of the bowl to one or two 1-cup
(237-ml)-size jars, as needed. Pack them down tightly and check the level of the brine.
If it hasn't come up above the level of the herbs, add salt brine with a ratio of
2 teaspoons (10 g) of salt to 1 cup (237 ml) water.

Weight down with a fermentation weight and cover the jar tightly. Ferment for 5 to
10 days or until tangy. Once fermentation is complete, transfer to cold storage.

Will keep for several weeks at room temperature, 2 to 3 months in a root cellar or up
to 6 months refrigerated.

Note: Green herbs oxidize—turn black—over time. This is a natural process and does
not harm the final product or shelf life of the herbs.

Soured Corn

Soured corn, like sauerkraut in Germany and kimchi in Korea, had a history in the South that I wasn't even aware of until recently. It makes sense, though, given that many foods ferment spontaneously or with very little effort. And corn, being a Southern staple long before industrialization, would have been utilized in every way possible by both the Native and Anglo Americans living in the South. This stuff is tangy and delicious and can be eaten raw to preserve its goodness, or, if you have large quantities that have been preserved through lactic acid fermentation, it can be fried up in a cast-iron skillet. I give the option to throw in a red bell pepper, mostly for color but also because they are often harvested around the same time.

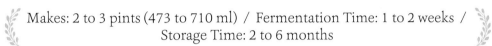

Makes: 2 to 3 pints (473 to 710 ml) / Fermentation Time: 1 to 2 weeks / Storage Time: 2 to 6 months

1 dozen ears sweet corn

1 red bell pepper, optional, mostly for color

1 quart (946 ml) water

3 tbsp (45 g) salt

Shuck the ears of corn and remove the kernels from the cob using a sharp knife. This is easiest to do by placing the ear of corn, stem-side down, in a pie pan or other wide, rimmed dish.

Pack the corn and red bell pepper into quart (1-L)- or pint (0.5 L)-size jars, leaving a couple of inches of headspace. Make a brine with the water and salt and pour it over the corn and peppers, making sure all of the corn is submerged.

Use a fermentation weight to weigh the corn down below the level of the brine. Seal the jars and allow to ferment for 1 to 2 weeks, or until sufficiently tangy, being sure to burp the jars daily to release any pent-up gas.

Move the jars to cold storage. Will keep at cool room temperature for 1 to 2 months. Keeps in a cellar or refrigerator for up to 6 months.

Pizza Green Beans

These pizza-inspired green beans have a great crunch and bold flavor. Serve them as you would a pickle at lunch, add them to a crudité platter or chop them up for a flavorful salad addition. The brine is also delicious when paired with olive oil for an Italian-inspired salad dressing.

Makes: 1 quart (946 ml) / Fermentation Time: At least 2 weeks / Storage Time: 2 to 12 months

1 tsp (5 g) dried oregano

1 garlic clove, peeled

Approximately 1 pint (200 g) green beans

2 small fresh tomatoes, diced

1½–2 tbsp (23–30 g) salt (more in warmer temperatures)

Water as needed

Add the dried oregano and garlic to the bottom of a quart (1-L) jar. Layer in half of the green beans and half of the diced tomatoes. Repeat with the remaining green beans and tomatoes up to the 3½-cup (830-ml) mark on the jar.

Add the salt and pour in enough water to cover all of the vegetables. Add the fermentation weight of your choosing (page 33) and seal the jar tightly.

Place at cool room temperature (60 to 80°F [16 to 27°C], optimally) and allow to ferment for at least two weeks. If you haven't used an airlock, then during this period, especially the first 5 to 7 days, you will need to burp the jars by quickly opening them to release the built-up gases that result from fermentation. To do so, carefully and quickly open the jar, listen for the release of gas and close the jar back up with just a bit of the gases still remaining inside.

After at least 2 weeks, move jar to cold storage or serve.

These will keep for several months at room temperature and 6 to 12 months in cold storage.

Beet and Turnip Sticks with Dill

Both turnips and beets have grown readily in our gardens but only beets are well-loved by our whole family. The strong flavor of turnips, especially as they grow, can be off-putting to children. So I like to combine them with foods I know we all like, as in the Homestead 'Chi (page 37) and this beet ferment. Since beets are higher in sugar, folks often shy away from fermenting them. Pairing them with sharp, low-sugar turnips results in a nice balance.

 Makes: 1 quart (946 ml) / Fermentation Time: 2 weeks / Fermentation Storage: 2 to 12 months

1 large turnip (softball size)

1 large beet (or 2 smaller)

¼ cup (7 g), packed, fresh dill

2½ tbsp (38 g) salt

Water as needed

Trim the turnip and cut into 4 sections from top to tail. Cut each of these into ½-inch (13-mm)-wide snacking sticks. Repeat with the beet.

Layer a quart (1-L) jar with alternating layers of turnip sticks, beet sticks and dill and salt, filling it just over three-quarters full. Pour filtered water over the vegetables until well covered and then add a fermentation weight. Seal the jar and allow to ferment at room temperature for 2 weeks, burping the jar daily as needed.

After 2 weeks, move the jar to cold storage or serve as a snack or crunchy addition to the dinner plate.

These beet and turnip sticks will keep for several months at cool room temperature and 6 to 12 months in cold storage.

Fruit Kraut

The only way to ferment fruit for long-term storage is to make alcohol with it. Otherwise you are better off dehydrating it and adding it to fermented beverages as needed. That is, unless you want to mix it into some kraut. Adding a small amount of fruit to cabbage results in a sweet, tangy, fizzy kraut while preserving that fruit for several months. The only caveat is that the fruit can easily produce yeasts and therefore molds, so be sure to rinse it off before using it and be vigilant about checking your jars.

 Makes: 2 quarts (1.9 L) / Fermentation Time: 2 to 3 weeks / Storage Time: 3 to 6 months

2 medium cabbages

1 apple

2 pints (606 g) blackberries

3 tbsp (45 g) salt

Shred the cabbage and apple as you would for coleslaw and combine in a large mixing bowl. Add the blackberries and salt and mix with your hands until all ingredients are well combined. Taste the mixture and make sure it has enough salt. It should taste like a fresh salad does when it is well-seasoned with salt. Add another sprinkling of salt if it is bland.

Pound the cabbage with a potato masher or kraut pounder. Alternatively, you can simply rub the salt into the cabbage and fruit with your hands until a bit of the liquid begins to come out of the cabbage.

Once the cabbage is limp and has begun to give off its juices, pack the kraut into two quart (1-L) jars or a half-gallon (2-L) jar, packing the jars up to approximately 3 cups (710 ml). Use your fist or a kitchen utensil to pack the kraut down into the jar as tightly as it will go so that the juices from the kraut come up above the level of the cabbage. If there is not enough brine to sufficiently cover the cabbage by at least 1 inch (25 mm), make additional brine by combining salt and water at a rate of ½ tablespoon (8 g) of salt per cup (237 ml) of water. Pour this over the kraut, leaving at least 1 to 2 inches (25 to 50 mm) of headspace.

Use a fermentation weight to weigh the cabbage down below the level of the brine. Seal the jars tightly and allow to ferment at cool room temperature (60 to 80°F [16 to 27°C]) for 2 to 3 weeks. During this time, check the jar for carbon dioxide build-up. If you notice bubbling or pressure building up, quickly burp the jar by loosening the lid just enough to release some of the gases, then quickly tighten it again.

Once the kraut is sufficiently fermented, transfer to cold storage.

Fruit kraut will keep at cool room temperature for up to 3 months and in cold storage for up to 6 months.

Kosher Dill Pickles

These pickles taste like the tangy canned cucumbers of my youth—full of garlic and dill flavor with just a hint of heat. Unlike those vinegar-brined pickles, however, these have a freshness to them that you simply cannot find in canned pickles. There is no better-loved pickle than this in our home.

 Makes: 1 half-gallon (1.9 L) / Fermentation Time: 1 to 3 weeks / Storage Time: 2 to 12 months

Large handful tannin-containing leaves (grape, oak, horseradish, mesquite, etc.)

1 tsp (5 g) red pepper flakes

Scant 2 quarts (1.9 L) pickling cucumbers

6 garlic cloves, peeled

2 large heads dill (or 4 tsp [2 g] dill weed or seed)

4½ tbsp (68 g) sea salt (5–6 tbsp [75–90 g] if fermenting at 85+°F [29+°C])

Water as needed

Add the tannin-containing leaves to the bottom of a half-gallon (2-L) vessel along with the red pepper flakes.

Fill the vessel one-third of the way with the cucumbers. Layer half of the garlic and dill. Repeat with another one-third of the cucumbers followed by the other half of the garlic and dill. Layer in the last one-third of the cucumbers, filling the jar approximately 80 percent of the way.

Pour the salt over the cucumbers, followed by the water. Fill the vessel with water, leaving approximately 1 inch (25 mm) of headspace. Use a fermentation weight to keep the cucumbers below the level of the brine, as needed. Seal the jar and leave at room temperature to ferment for 1 to 3 weeks or until the cucumbers are tart and the brine is cloudy. Be sure to burp the jar daily, especially during the first week of fermentation, so as to avoid a buildup of gases.

Transfer to cold storage. Will keep for 2 to 4 months at cool room temperature (60 to 80°F [16 to 27°C], optimally) or 4 to 12 months in a cool cellar or refrigerator.

Fermented Fresh Shelling Beans

We pick black-eyed peas at three stages. The first is the green bean stage when we eat them just as we would string beans. In the final stage the beans and pods are both dried and can be stored either as dried beans or used for next year's seed. In between, there is the golden shelling bean stage when the beans are both starchy and fresh. Combining these with plenty of herbs and garden vegetables makes for a stellar, very active ferment. Beans contain a prebiotic fiber that makes this ferment very "alive," so be sure to check frequently for burping.

Makes: 2 quarts (1.9 L) / Fermentation Time: 1 to 2 weeks / Storage Time: Up to 2 months

2½ cups (375 g) freshly shelled black-eyed peas or other field bean

1 medium cucumber, chopped

1 cup (40 g) packed, roughly chopped cilantro

1 large carrot, chopped

2 medium tomatoes, chopped

½ red onion, minced

1 cup (40 g) packed, roughly chopped parsley

3 garlic cloves, minced

2–3 tbsp (30–45 g) salt

Water to cover

Combine all ingredients in a large bowl. Mix well to combine. Transfer to two quart (1 L) jars, packing them until they are a little more than three-quarters full. Cover the vegetables with water as needed and add sufficient fermentation weights.

Seal jar tightly and allow to ferment for 1 to 2 weeks, burping daily as needed. Transfer to cold storage or serve. Keeps for 1 month at room temperature or 2 months in cold storage.

Sweet Potato Chips with Dried Chilies

July through September brings triple-digit daytime temperatures, restless warm nights and little rainfall to our Texas homestead. Not surprisingly, those Southern staples of black-eyed peas, okra, collard greens and sweet potatoes are about all that hold on through these tough months. The fall sweet potato harvest is always exciting, and we like to store the potatoes for a couple of months before roasting, baking, frying and stewing them. These fermented sweet potato chips are very active and need to be eaten quickly as their high starch content can soon become yeasty. But they make for a delicious, if short-lived, snack.

 Makes: 1 quart (946 ml) / Fermentation Time: 2 weeks / Storage Time: Up to 2 months

3 small sweet potatoes

2 tbsp (30 g) sea salt

1 tsp (3 g) cumin seeds

A small handful of tannin leaves

2 dried chilies (ancho, poblano, etc.)

Water, as needed

Cut the sweet potatoes in half lengthwise and then into thin slices. Mix the sweet potatoes with salt, seeds and tannin leaves in a medium bowl. Break the chilies into 2 pieces so that there are 4 chile pieces altogether.

In a quart (1 L) jar, layer one-fourth of sweet potato mixture with 1 piece of chile. Repeat with remaining sweet potatoes and chilies until the jar is just over three-quarters full. Pour in water to cover vegetables. Add a fermentation weight and seal the jar tightly.

Allow to ferment at room temperature for 2 weeks, burping the jar daily as needed. Transfer to cold storage for 1 to 2 months or consume within 1 to 2 weeks if storing at room temperature.

Everyday Spicy Carrots

Only once have I fermented homegrown carrot sticks. We had such a glut of them and the weather turned wet and warm, so we needed to harvest them before they began to rot. Generally, we eat homegrown carrots so fast that there is simply no need. This recipe is an everyday snack made from organic carrots I pick up at the grocery store. It keeps us eating fermented veggies even when the gardens are low, and they are a simple, inexpensive source of probiotics. Now I can speak from experience to say using homegrown carrots results in the tastiest, most alive version of this ferment.

 Makes: 1 quart (946 ml) / Fermentation Time: 1 to 3 weeks / Storage Time: 2 to 12 months

3 garlic cloves, peeled

¼–½ tsp red pepper flakes, depending on heat preference

Approximately 1½ lb (0.68 kg) carrots

1 tbsp (15 g) salt (2 tbsp [30 g] if fermenting at 80+°F [27+°C])

Water as needed

Add the garlic cloves and red pepper flakes to the bottom of a quart (1-L) jar.

Chop the carrots into thin sticks just long enough to fit standing vertically below the neck of the jar, keeping in mind that thinner carrot sticks ferment faster.

Add the salt to the carrots and pour in water to cover the carrots, leaving about 1 inch (25 mm) of headspace. If your carrot sticks are very small, use a fermentation weight to submerge them.

Seal the jar and place at cool room temperature (60 to 80°F [16 to 27°C], optimally) to ferment for 7 to 21 days, or until the carrots are quite tangy. Be sure to burp the jar at least once per day for the first 10 days during the fermentation time.

Move to cold storage. Will keep for up to 2 months at room temperature and 6 to 12 months in a cellar or refrigerator.

Whole Fermented Peppers and Sauce

If you have an abundance of peppers to preserve, you could not choose an easier method. The result is stunning both visually and gastronomically speaking. I prefer to ferment the whole peppers, which keep for a long time, and then blend them as needed for hot sauce, which doesn't keep as long once blended.

Makes: 2 quarts (1.9 L) / Fermentation Time: At least 3 weeks / Storage Time: 3 to 12 months

2 garlic cloves

1 lb (0.45 kg) sweet peppers

3 jalapeños

3 tbsp (45 g) sea salt

Water to cover

Add the garlic cloves to the bottom of a half-gallon (2-L) jar or two quart (1-L) jars. Layer in the sweet and jalapeño peppers, packing down loosely. Add the salt and cover the vegetables with water. Add the fermentation weight of your choosing (page 33) and seal the jar(s) tightly.

Place at cool room temperature (60 to 80°F [16 to 27°C], optimally) and allow to ferment for at least 3 weeks. If you haven't used an airlock, then during this period, especially during the first 5 to 7 days, you will need to burp the jars by quickly opening them to release the built-up gases that result from fermentation. To do so, carefully and quickly open the jar, listen for the release of gas and close the jar back up with just a bit of the gases still remaining inside.

Whole fermented peppers will keep at room temperature for several months or in cold storage for 6 to 12 months.

To make a mild hot sauce, blend the peppers with brine in a blender or work them through a food mill. For a true hot sauce, substitute hot peppers for at least half of the sweet peppers. Ferment as recommended and proceed with recipe as written.

Serve the peppers whole as a snack or a side or serve the blended sauce with meat, mixed into a salad dressing or tossed into a cold grain salad.

Whole Fermented Tomatoes

In high summer, when both the temperatures and the garden haul soar to new heights, food preservation needs to be as simple as possible. This simple ferment allows you to put up loads of tomatoes in a simple brine solution so you can use them in salads, sauces and snacks later. There is no other means of preserving tomatoes that I know of that requires so little time and effort.

Makes: 1 quart (946 ml) / Fermentation Time: 3 to 4 weeks / Storage Time: Up to 12 months

1 lb (0.45 kg) small to medium tomatoes

3 tbsp (45 g) salt (2 tbsp [30 g] if fermenting at 85°F or below)

Water to cover

Pack tomatoes into a quart (1-L) jar, leaving approximately 2 inches (50 mm) of headspace. Add salt and cover tomatoes with filtered water. Use a fermentation weight to keep the tomatoes below the level of the brine.

Cover the jar tightly and leave to ferment at room temperature for 3 to 4 weeks. During this time, check the jar for carbon dioxide buildup. If you notice bubbling or pressure building up in the jar, quickly burp it by loosening the lid just enough to release some of the gases and then quickly tighten it again.

Once the tomatoes and brine are sufficiently fermented, transfer the jar to cold storage. Serve tomatoes as you would a pickle, or blend to create Raw Fermented Marinara Sauce (see page 214).

Fermented tomatoes will keep for several months at cool room temperature or 6 to 12 months in cold storage.

Basic Brine-Fermented Vegetables

Making fermented vegetables out of whatever you've got is critical to making lactic acid fermentation sustainable in the long term. These recipes, therefore, are intended to be used as a road map to ferment and preserve whatever you harvest, procure locally or purchase at the grocery store.

Good candidates for this ferment are whole or large pieces of cucumbers, peppers, tomatoes, carrots, eggplant sticks, broccoli, cauliflower, green beans, okra, beets, turnips and radishes.

 Makes: 2 quarts (2 L) / Fermentation Time: 2 to 6 weeks / Storage Time: Up to 12 months

Garlic, herbs or pickling spices as desired

Large handful of tannin-containing leaves (oak, grape, mesquite, horseradish, etc.)

Enough vegetables, whole or cut no thicker than 1 inch (25 mm), to fill a half-gallon (2-L) jar (approximately 3½ pints)

3–6 tbsp (45–90 g) sea salt (3 tbsp [45 g] for cooler, 4½ tbsp [68 g] for moderately warm, 6 tbsp [90 g] for hot)

Water as needed

Place the garlic, herbs or pickling spices into the half-gallon jar. Add the tannin-containing leaves on top. Pack the jar tightly with whatever vegetable or combination of vegetables needs preserving. Fill to a little bit below the neck of the jar, approximately 80 percent full.

Pour the salt over the vegetables and cover the vegetables with water, filling the jar up to 1 inch (25 mm) from the rim. Weight down with a fermentation weight so the brine covers the vegetables.

Seal the jar and place at cool room temperature (60–80°F [16–27°C], optimally) to ferment for 2 to 6 weeks, burping the jar to release pent-up gases for the first 1 to 2 weeks. After the first 1 to 2 weeks you can move the ferments to a cooler cellar (45 to 60°F [7 to 16°C]) if you wish to slow down the process and keep them in long-term storage. If your cellar is around 60°F (16°C), you can allow the vegetables to ferment in the cellar from the start, though it would take a bit of time to get the pH down. You would also have to make once- or twice-daily treks to the cellar to burp the jars.

If utilizing refrigeration, move the ferments to the refrigerator after the vegetables are pleasantly tangy, 2 to 6 weeks.

Basic Self-Brining Fermented Vegetables

Unlike the previous recipe, these types of vegetables are grated and sliced thin to create as much surface area as possible to form a brine from the vegetables' own moisture.

Good candidates for this type of ferment include grated or thinly sliced cabbage, carrots, turnips, beets (when cut with lower-sugar vegetables), collard greens, kale, herbs, summer squash, cucumbers and radishes.

 Makes: 1 quart (946 ml) / Fermentation Time: 2 to 6 weeks / Storage Time: Up to 12 months

Garlic, herbs or pickling spices as desired

Approximately 4 cups (1,360 g) grated or thinly sliced vegetables or 1 medium cabbage, thinly sliced

2–4 tbsp (30–60 g) salt per quart (1 L)

1 cup (237 ml) water plus 1½ tsp (8 g) salt, as needed

In a large bowl, combine the garlic, herbs or pickling spices with the grated or chopped vegetables and the salt. Pound with a kraut pounder or potato masher or massage with your hands briefly, cover with a heavy plate and leave for approximately 1 hour for the salt to draw out the natural moisture.

Pack the jars with vegetables, using clean hands or a mallet to tightly pack vegetables and avoid air pockets. Fill the jar approximately 80 percent full and place a fermentation weight on top of the vegetables to keep them below the level of the brine. If the vegetables have not produced sufficient brine, mix the water and salt as indicated for a brine and pour over the vegetables up to 1 inch (25 mm) from the rim of the jar.

Seal the jar and place at cool room temperature (60 to 80°F [16 to 27°C], optimally) to ferment for 2 to 6 weeks, burping the jar to release pent-up gases for the first 1 to 2 weeks. After the first 1 to 2 weeks, you can move the ferments to a cooler cellar (45 to 60°F [7 to 16°C]) if you wish to slow down the process and keep them in long-term storage. If your cellar is around 60°F (16°C), you can allow them to ferment in the cellar from the start, though it would take a bit of time to get the pH down. You would also have to make once- or twice-daily treks to the cellar to burp the jars.

If utilizing refrigeration, move the ferments to the refrigerator after the vegetables are pleasantly tangy, 2 to 6 weeks.

Triple-Ferment Potato Salad

Many times fermented foods are snuck into meals to mask their flavor or hide them from those we wish to feed well. That doesn't have to be the case, though. This recipe is a shining reminder that fermented foods can be used for flavor, texture and that certain lactic acid punch that vinegar and pasteurized pickles simply can't provide. Not only beautiful, this potato salad was once declared "the best" by my husband whom I affectionally call the grocery store potato salad connoisseur.

 Makes: 6 to 8 servings

2½ lb (1.1 kg) russet potatoes, washed

5 hardboiled eggs

3 large celery ribs, chopped

½ large red onion, minced

½ cup (170 g) sauerkraut or other Basic Self-Brining Vegetable (page 63), packed

¼ cup (85 g) Kosher Dill Pickles (page 51) or Everyday Spicy Carrots (page 56), minced

¾ cup (180 ml) Veg Brine Mayonnaise (page 205) or other good-quality mayonnaise

2 tbsp (30 ml) apple cider vinegar, or more to taste

2 tbsp (5 g) fresh, minced dill

2 tbsp (30 ml) prepared mustard

2 tbsp (30 ml) olive oil

Salt and pepper to taste

Place the potatoes in a Dutch oven and cover them with water. Cover the pot, place it over high heat and bring to a boil. Reduce the heat to medium-low, generously salt the pot, and simmer for 15 to 25 minutes, or until just fork tender. Drain the potatoes and set aside to cool.

Meanwhile, peel the hardboiled eggs and slice them in half lengthwise. Chop each egg half into 8 pieces and add them to a large mixing or serving bowl. Add the celery, onion, sauerkraut and chopped pickles to the diced egg. Once the potatoes are cool enough to handle, chop them into large bite-size pieces and add them to the egg-vegetable mixture. Stir gently to combine all of the ingredients.

Combine the mayonnaise, vinegar, dill, mustard and olive oil in a pint (0.5-L)-size jar with an air-tight lid. Shake well to combine. Pour this dressing over the other ingredients and sprinkle generously with salt and pepper. Stir to combine all ingredients. Taste and adjust seasoning as needed. If serving immediately, more vinegar may also be needed.

Serve immediately or cover and refrigerate for several hours or up to 2 days. Before serving, stir in any liquid that may have separated from the salad and adjust seasoning as needed.

Five Ingredient or Less Kimchi Noodles

This flavorful dish is one of the simplest to make and uses a great deal of one of our favorite ferments. Serve it with or without meat for a quick meal full of the goodness of fermented vegetables.

 Makes: 4 to 6 servings

1 lb (454 g) pasta (gluten-free works)

1 lb (454 g) meat (optional)

Salt and pepper to taste

2 cups (680 g), packed, Homestead 'Chi (page 37)

3-4 tbsp (44-59 ml) Homestead 'Chi brine

8 green onions, green parts only, chopped

Cook the noodles according to the package directions or until al dente. Drain and rinse to remove some of the starch. If using ground beef or chicken, cook until browned and cooked completely through. Season the meat with salt and pepper to taste and set aside to cool.

Once the noodles and meat are both cooled to at least room temperature, combine them in a serving bowl with the Homestead 'Chi, the kimchi brine, the green onions and a pinch of salt. Toss all ingredients together and taste for seasoning. Season with salt and more brine to taste.

Grains

In the hottest of months, I waddled across a dirt path, passing chickens and mesquite trees on my way to the first home our family knew on these two acres. I was pregnant when we first moved into that camper, just as I was this August day. Three years and two babies later, we had moved into the homemade cabin that had no oven. My solar oven baking was mediocre at best, with a steep learning curve I hadn't mastered, so that tiny camper oven was my bakery until a larger propane stove came our way.

Why I was baking on a triple-digit day with a belly over which I could not see my shoes I can only explain in one word—sourdough. Although we were attempting to surround ourselves with homegrown and homemade food and community, we lived in a bit of a real-food black hole. It became clear very quickly that if we wanted good bread—good *anything*, really—we were going to have to make it ourselves.

For years prior to this, we didn't eat any grains at all. We tried to heal our guts by eating mostly meat, vegetables, ferments and broth. It helped quite a bit, actually. And then we moved to our homestead where the manual labor increased drastically and little boys became big eaters, so grains made their way back in. As is often the case, we ended up sliding into convenient habits. Without electricity or a sink big enough to wash a mixing bowl, I sometimes opted to just buy that loaf of processed bread. Not long after things began to go downhill with suspected gluten intolerance, a reminder of the importance of fermentation and making one's own food.

When our off-grid kitchen was built, and our countertops and cabinets reflected the seven people we fed three times per day, I had no more excuses. I made a natural sourdough starter for gluten-free baking. I let oats bubble away on the counter for days—or until I remembered them. We ate tangy porridge with kefir and eventually fermented wheat breads from organic flour. What we once avoided became nourishment for a growing family.

Anyone who ferments is a maker, a nurturer, a steward. We must take what is given to us and make the most of it, knowing always that with those gifts come responsibility. Fermentation does just that for grains—it brings out the best of the seed, utilizes it for nourishment of the body, and feeds the ones who tend the land, which brings forth the seed once again.

It is symbiotic; a closed cycle … until that cycle breaks down. The breakdown happened, I believe, when we, as a culture, moved away from the land. When you frequently germinate seeds, you understand that water and warmth are necessary for the plant's optimal growth and health; that through this process, a transformation from seed to edible food occurs. The same goes for the seeds we call grain—water and warmth turn a hard, dormant seed into life-giving nourishment. But if we step away from that picture and lose an understanding of how food comes to be, the importance seems irrelevant and the cycle of symbiosis breaks down.

I suspect that is where we are today: bread as the enemy, fear and loathing in the dough. As is often the case, I believe the way forward is to look back to the old paths, back to naturally leavened sourdough breads.

SOURDOUGH: THE NUTRITIONAL, SUSTAINABLE WAY FORWARD

Most of the bread available today—even so-called "sourdough" breads—are made from commercial yeast. Up until very recently, historically speaking, this was not the case. To understand the importance of natural leavening, let us take a closer look at its modern industrialized counterpart.

The Origin and Application of Commercial Yeast

Commercial yeast was created out of a desire to both make baking more predictable—a necessity for large-scale production—and to cut down on the time necessary to make bread by natural means—a cost-cutting factor. When bread is made outside of the home or community, a large-scale baking model requires corners to be cut to keep costs down.

Yeast itself is not a chemically derived entity; it occurs everywhere in nature. It is in the air we breathe, it is in our bodies, it exists in food, drink, soil and animals. Yeast is what makes wine and beer what it is; historical accounts of beer making and bread baking often happening in tandem. The grains that were fermented for beer produced various bacteria, acids and yeasts, the latter of which was desirable for making bread. And so the home or town baker would use a bit of the dregs of yeast from the bottom of the bottle or the foaming yeast of the brew, depending on which stage in the process the beer was at when you needed to make bread. These yeasts were then used much like a sourdough starter to slowly leaven the bread into a loaf fermented not only by the yeasts, but also by the other bacteria present.

Commercial yeast is a convenience food; the isolation of one component from its natural matrix. Like a vitamin taken from food and isolated into a pill or the extraction of corn syrup from an ear of corn, it is an unnatural seclusion that would not exist outside a highly processed industrial food system. In other words, no one makes B vitamin pills or corn syrup from items foraged in their backyard. Just as highly processed "foods" have been shown to wreak havoc on the human body, baking with commercial yeast is not without consequence. Namely, there is a lack of fermentation in the bread and the art and science of sourdough baking is lost.

And to put this into context: For pretty much all of the history of bread making before the mid- to late-nineteenth century, bread was made with natural leavening that gave the dough time to ferment while it rose. Breads made with commercial yeast are, therefore, a modern, industrialized food.

The Nutritional Importance of Grain Fermentation in a Post-Industrial Food System

Without refrigeration, grains and other foods begin to ferment spontaneously. Therefore, soaked millet begins to sour, and a bowl of flour and water begins to bubble if simply given time and warmth. You can imagine, then, that this is how bread came to be—a bit of dough left a bit too long becomes risen dough, for instance.

To be clear, there absolutely *are* examples of healthy ancient people groups that consumed whole, unfermented grains.

They generally also consumed so much nutrient-dense animal and plant food that grains were somewhat minimal in the diet and nutrient density far outweighed any negative effects of the grain. Their grain was also not chemically treated, hybridized over generations for mechanized farming, or genetically modified for higher yields.

Context is important. Knowing that it is possible to eat whole, unfermented grains and still maintain good health is not necessarily a reason *not* to ferment grains. The dietary and lifestyle context of those people groups eating unfermented grain is a world away from the post-GMO, post-chemicalized, post-industrialized agriculture world we currently live in. That doesn't even mention the disparity from then to now in areas like gut-compromising antibiotics and pharmaceuticals, hormone-laden animal products and hugely depleted soil makeups. To say that we now live in a time when we need our food to *give* our bodies more than it *takes* is a great understatement.

Nutritionally, fermentation is a sort of pre-digestion. Complex sugars and fibers are broken down, giving our bodies less digestive toil. As described in a 2008 study on sourdough bread entitled "Starch Digestibility and Postprandial Glycemic Response," simple starches are digested and converted by lactobacilli into a food with far less impact on our blood sugar than both the original grain and the loaves leavened by commercial yeast. This food also multiplies the vitamin content and allows the body to absorb naturally occurring minerals in the grain due to the neutralizing of mineral-chelating agents through the fermentation process.

Fermentation is especially important if you desire to consume whole grains. Although we have been taught that whole grains are better for us, we have not been told that most healthy, ancient societies who ate whole-grain bread did not have access to fast-rising commercial yeast and therefore ate long-fermented loaves. We are not told that some of the more difficult-to-digest constituents in grain come in the very parts that are removed during refining. We are not told that some ancient societies actually went the extra step of sifting out the bran when they were making unleavened, unfermented flat breads. And we were certainly not told of the vitamin and mineral deficiencies, the belly aches and the fatigue when, through trade, grains were brought to new corners of the world while the wisdom of how to prepare them was left behind.

Anecdotally, I have seen the difference in our own family in the eight years since I began fermenting our grains. Pancakes don't sit like lead bricks when they're given twelve hours with the sourdough starter. Bread does not bloat nor does it demand you eat slice after slice when it has risen slowly, allowing the lactobacilli to go to work on the grain, breaking down sugars and increasing the B vitamins in the process. We don't feel tired after a bowl of organic oats that bubbled for 24 hours before being cooked and served with milk kefir. Of the many scientific studies and ancient food practices I have read in the past decade, observing the impact of fermented grains on my family is the most convincing, and it is the reason I forge ahead with this practice.

THE SUSTAINABLE SOURDOUGH STARTER

In the context of sustainability for the home baker, commercial yeast reminds me a bit of hybrid seeds—you can use them but you'll never really gain independence by doing so. And what are the consequences of using something as unnatural as a seed that does not grow true or a yeast that does not ferment naturally?

Every year, we try to save seed from at least a few of the vegetables we grow, always hoping to expand our collection and reduce the number of heirloom seed packets we purchase. By saving seed, we are adapting plants to our local climate, its growing conditions and the many aspects of sun, rain and temperature that make up the health and production of a plant. In doing so, we tend to get hardier plants for our area and vegetables that can handle the extremes found in *our region*. It also allows us a bit of self-sufficiency in that we do not need to earn the money to purchase the seed to grow the vegetables. We have, instead, produced the seed ourselves from the same land from whence the vegetables came.

Likewise, a sourdough starter made from flour and water is homegrown yeast. If you are able to grow the grain yourself, the only outside ingredient you might need for good bread is salt. Not only that, you are creating a bread culture with organisms very particular to your area—a concept called terroir. Literally translated, this French word means land. In the artisanal food movement, it refers to the soil, climate and inputs specific to a region that give a wine, cheese or bread its character. These foods cannot be mimicked by industrial means.

Whether you are looking for three-ingredient bread, the end of buying yeast or easy-to-digest morning toast; fermented grains and bread can solve a lot of problems in the kitchen.

To get started, you'll need to understand how to make a sourdough starter from just two simple ingredients. If you can master keeping a sourdough starter happy and imbibed with a large colony of bacteria and yeasts, you will have fought and won much of the seemingly daunting battle of having everyday fermented bread.

The Keeping Quality of Sourdough

Have you ever read the ingredient list on a loaf of commercially produced bread and wondered why in the world all of those extra hard-to-pronounce ingredients are necessary? A lot of them are preservatives—they give bread a longer shelf life.

Between the lower pH and the microbial activity in sourdough bread, it is no surprise that bakers and scientists alike are finding that sourdough bread keeps much better than breads made solely with commercial yeast. In fact, one 2012 study entitled "The Effect of Sourdough and Calcium Propionate on the Microbial Shelf Life of Salt-Reduced Bread" found that a common food preservative, calcium propionate, could be replaced with natural sourdough fermentation resulting in an improvement in keeping quality.

Once you make the switch from commercial yeast baking to naturally fermented sourdough baking, you will find that your bread doesn't go stale as quickly and that the bread's flavor and texture are consistent for days after baking.

SOURDOUGH STARTER: THE MAIN INGREDIENT

A good loaf of naturally leavened bread lives or dies by its sourdough starter. All other ingredients matter, of course, but an unhealthy starter is a sure way to create mediocre loaves at best, and to lose heart quickly when you are just starting out. If this has been your experience, there is a good chance that you have either been given poor instructions or your sourdough starter is simply not up to snuff.

For a robust starter that leavens bread well and lends great flavor and aroma to bread, the sourdough culture must be given what it needs. So let's take a closer look at the sourdough starter's constituents and how to encourage great baking results.

The Microbial Makeup of a Sourdough Starter

Ironically enough, I am forever skeptical of all things claiming the title "science." For me, personally, seeing the natural process of bubbling sourdough starter, which converts flour and water into something delicious and nutritious, was all the evidence I needed to dive into natural leavening.

But I'm also forever asking how and why, so I can't quite help myself when it comes to understanding what is really going on during the fermentation process. As I have come to understand the broadest sense of the biological phenomena, I have become more comfortable with baking without recipes. The biological understanding, therefore, begets the artisanal baking, at least in my case.

A sourdough starter is teeming with all sorts of microbial life. Focusing on five of these elements will aid you in understanding how the process really works.

Bacteria are generally the first on the scene when water and flour are combined. The most commonly noted bacterium is lactobacilli, though there are others. Eventually, through frequent feedings and aeration, yeasts begin to multiply and take hold.

Yeasts and bacteria are therefore the backbone of a sourdough starter. But it is the by-products of a starter that do some of the most recognized work.

Lactic acid is one of the organic acids produced by the bacteria present in a sourdough starter. It gives sourdough its tang, of course, but it also works on the dough as it ferments to create a tender crumb much like adding buttermilk to biscuits or pancakes.

Enzymes are also present during this process and play a critical role in the dough. The enzymes split the starches and convert them to sugars, a food easily feasted upon by the bacteria and yeasts. They also break down proteins in the process.

Carbon dioxide is the final major component and is a by-product of the fermentation. This gas is trapped in the matrix of the bread dough, increasing the volume of the dough and creating a light loaf rather than a hard brick.

It is important to note that much of the process of sourdough fermentation is based on the symbiosis that exists between all of these constituents. Certain yeasts do their best work when the pH is reduced by the organic acids that are produced by the bacteria, for instance.

How to Encourage Yeast Activity for Less Sour, Higher-Rising Bread

Of the many organic constituents of a sourdough starter, the yeast component is the most sought after. The bacteria produce the acids and break down the fibers and starches, but the yeast is what we are after for a fluffy, well-risen loaf. Generally speaking, bacteria are much more prolific than yeast in a starter and when a starter is neglected, the bacteria tend to take over even more so.

So the question becomes how can we, in the care of our sourdough starter, tip the balance of the culture in favor of yeasts rather than bacteria? These types of starters produce well-risen bread with good crumb and a delicate balance of tang. Here are some tips:

1. Feed a High Ratio of Flour to the Starter

In old French recipes I have come across, they often talk of building the *levain,* or leavening. They do not simply use a cup of the sourdough culture. Instead, they take a few spoons of that mother culture and add it to a cup or more of flour with enough water to make a slurry. In this scenario, a small amount of culture is introduced to a large amount of flour. The high starch content that yeast colonies love is followed in rapid succession by yeast proliferation and moderate bacterial proliferation.

This can be achieved through one of two means. You can, as was often done in old-time bakeries, simply build a levain before baking. Approximately eight to twelve hours before baking, use a small amount of your starter culture to inoculate the flour and water necessary to build the amount of starter you will need for a recipe. Feed your mother starter and set it aside, then proceed with your recipe using the levain as the sourdough starter ingredient.

Alternatively, you can feed your sourdough starter frequently with large quantities of fresh flour and water in relation to the starter. This does, of course, create a problem. Either you end up with a very large quantity of starter or you must discard starter frequently. For ways in which to use discarded starter, see page 81.

2. Aerate the Sourdough Starter

Yeasts are especially fond of oxygen and, although a good initial stir gets the ball rolling, frequent and even oxygen exposure can really boost the yeast population—and therefore the leavening ability—of a sourdough starter. This is true for both wheat and gluten-free sourdough starters. My advice is to try giving your starter a vigorous stir a few times per day if you are keeping it on the counter. If you decide to refrigerate your starter, give it a daily stir and/or give it a few stirs while you are allowing it to come to room temperature in preparation for baking. You will be surprised at how much of a difference this makes.

Leavening Bread Naturally Without a Sourdough Starter

Though all of the recipes in this chapter utilize sourdough starter as the leavening agent, there are other natural yeast options available.

Kombucha, milk kefir and water kefir are all full of yeasts and can be used to inoculate or directly ferment bread. Either start your sourdough starter with a bit of one of these guys or mix the dough up using one as the liquid. Just keep an eye on your bread, as the rise time may differ from that of a sourdough-leavened bread.

Fruit yeasts are an interesting way of collecting and creating homemade yeast. They are essentially much like a Dried Fruit Kvass (page 186) in that dried fruit contributes its innate bacteria to a few cups of water. Add ¼ cup (38 g) of organic raisins to a quart (946 ml) of water. Fill to the 3-cup (720-ml) mark with filtered water, cover loosely and leave to ferment. After several days in warm temperatures, the water begins to bubble, indicating that the yeast is ready to be harvested.

From there you can create a pre-ferment by combining this yeast water with flour. Let it ferment eight to twelve hours and you now essentially have a sourdough starter that can be used in baking. The longer fermentation times needed when baking with a sourdough starter are much the same as when using a fruit yeast starter.

CREATING A SOURDOUGH RHYTHM THAT WORKS FOR YOU

What some see as a drawback to sourdough baking–long rise times–I actually see as a positive. With commercial yeast, you often have the bulk ferment, final rise and baking period all in the matter of a couple of hours. It can be a little too intense, if you have other things going on during that time period. Sourdough baking, on the other hand, often has a period of four to twelve hours between steps.

By getting your hands-on work out of the way at the right moment, sourdough can become a slow and easy process, done on your schedule. The trick is in planning things just right.

With my schedule, I like to do an overnight bulk ferment. Then, first thing in the morning, I shape, rise and bake loaves that will last us a couple of days. Many of our staple recipes–Wheat Sourdough Sandwich Bread (page 84), Quintessential Sourdough Farm Loaf (page 88) and Gluten-Free Sourdough Seeded Country Loaf (page 107)–are all good examples of that strategy.

For days when I know I'll be home and want to make something special, I anchor the 4- to 6-hour steps to meal times. Before breakfast I start the bulk ferment, after lunch I proceed with the next step and around suppertime the bread is ready to rise. Once you've mastered these recipes, you can mold them to your own schedule.

If it is available to you, you can use refrigeration as a tool to work sourdough into your schedule. Putting a dough into the refrigerator greatly extends the time between steps. So, if you are doing an eight-hour bulk ferment on the counter, you could instead leave it on the counter for one to two hours and then transfer it to the refrigerator for twelve or more hours. The cold of the refrigerator slows the fermentation process.

EMBRACING THE UNPREDICTABLE NATURE OF NATURAL LEAVENING

Because fermentation is dependent on the environment surrounding it, all fermentation recipes depend, to a great extent, on the ability of the fermenter to be truly present throughout the process. Sourdough baking is only black-and-white when all elements are always equal–from the microbial makeup of the starter to the room temperature to the water temperature. Since these things are not always equal, reading your dough is actually more important than reading your recipe.

You can become content with the unpredictability of sourdough baking if you are willing to feel the dough beneath your fingers and understand what it is that makes one batch differently from the next. There are several factors that can make a recipe turn out differently from one day to the next:

1. The temperature during all periods of fermentation.

2. The state of your sourdough starter, how recently and often it has been fed and what other microbes may be in your kitchen.

3. The fat, salt and sugar content of your dough.

A baker like myself actually thrives under these conditions—baking that has no hard-and-fast rules. I personally prefer to understand the process and then work within larger parameters to achieve a great loaf rather than simply follow a recipe that depends on just the right ingredients and environment. (How does one achieve such persnickety consistency in a real home kitchen, anyway?)

I understand, however, that the very nature of sourdough—the need to bob and weave when necessary—is quite maddening to some. If this is you, then simply do what you can to control your environment and your starter. Consistency in feeding times, ingredients and temperature will give you the least variable results, as can this little tip:

Sourdough fermentation slows down in the presence of salt and fat. If you are working in warmer-than-average conditions, consider adding fat and a tiny bit of extra salt to your dough or simply choose one of the richer recipes like the Wheat Sourdough Sandwich Loaf (page 84) or Wheat Sourdough Crescent Rolls (page 87). If you are working in cooler-than-average conditions, a lean dough will give you a faster rise time.

If there is one place where you can firmly plant your roots, it is in knowing the *process* of sourdough baking rather than the recipe. Feel the dough to adjust moisture, watch your starter and aerate when necessary and judge a rising time by the look of your dough rather than a clock on the wall.

THE LONG AND SHORT OF LONG FERMENTATION

It takes time, they say, for just about anything worthwhile. As for good bread with loads of flavor and easy digestibility, time is the ultimate ingredient. It is through time that fermentation does its work, breaking down fibers, converting starches and creating a loaf that is nourishing enough to serve every day.

This is why I prefer to give dough at least twelve hours of fermentation total, if not a bit more. It is possible to over-ferment bread because eventually glutens begin to break down too much and the enzyme action has converted too much of the starch. Over-fermented dough feels slack and doesn't take shape very well. It also does not rise well, lacks oven spring and tends to have an imbalance of flavor.

Some bakers ferment their dough for days... but they do so with the aid of refrigeration. A long, slow fermentation is the most desirable for all aspects of flavor and nourishment but *a moderate fermentation of twelve to eighteen hours at room temperature is usually at the intersection of doable and digestible.*

THE GLUTEN QUESTION

There has been much ado about gluten in the previous decade, and for good reason. A lot of people have found that they simply feel better when they don't eat wheat. I can understand that because I, and others in my family, have gone through a similar experience.

In our times away from gluten, I have learned three things:

1. Most wheat is sprayed with chemicals, especially glyphosate, as part of the commercial wheat production process. Glyphosate has now been found to mimic symptoms of gluten intolerance and cause a host of other health issues. Clean, organically grown wheat is important, as is knowing how truly organic it is because some organic wheat has been found to be contaminated with glyphosate as well.

2. Fermentation makes most things easier to digest, including the gluten found in wheat. Because sourdough fermentation unlocks enzymes that go to work on breaking down proteins (gluten), this makes sense. In fact, a 2010 study entitled "Gluten-Free Sourdough Wheat Baked Goods Appear Safe for Young Celiac Patients: A Pilot Study" and others have been widely touted as evidence of the benefits of bread fermentation for those with gluten sensitivity. A long, slow fermentation is critical in breaking down such proteins, however, and, of course, all caution should be exercised for those with severe symptoms or full-blown celiac disease.

3. We like bread enough to spend a bit of time on it. Much of the difficulty with wheat is that we rush something that is meant to be a slow and meaningful process. To mix dough and let it ferment for 12 to 24 hours does not take a whole lot of effort, but it is very valuable for those of us who want real bread that is truly nourishing.

But if long fermentation of organic wheat still creates a bread that leaves you feeling less than ideal, don't eat it. Listening to your body is probably your best bet.

GLUTEN-FREE SOURDOUGH BAKING

With all of this talk of fermentation making wheat digestible and you should just give it a try, you would think this whole chapter would be on wheat-based breads. The irony of the situation is that I have actually done a lot of gluten-free baking and the gluten-free sourdough breads in this chapter are a testament to my desire for great bread despite a wheat-free diet.

I think it is important to recognize that some people simply cannot tolerate some foods, and wheat is one of them. It's also historically relevant to point out that many, many cultures had no access to wheat and yet still survived just fine on fermented grains of all different varieties.

Grains like rye, barley, buckwheat and millet have sustained cultures as a caloric staple when wheat was too expensive or too scarce for those outside of aristocracy to afford its use. Having stood in a golden field of wheat, and threshed and winnowed the grain by hand, this homesteader might choose to dig potatoes for supper rather than go through the many steps it takes to turn that grain into a precious loaf of sourdough bread. For that reason, grains like corn, millet and buckwheat appeal more to me for all aspects of their growth and food preparation, including the ease in which the grain itself is removed from the plant.

If alternative grains appeal to you because you can grow and harvest them more readily, or because wheat is not an option for you, take heart in knowing that these grains can be fermented and used in sourdough baking with delicious results. Indeed, they already have been.

Buckwheat is incorporated into crepes in areas of France and teff into *injera* in Ethiopia, and fermented millet porridge is a staple food in Africa and Asia. None of these recipes ask gluten-free grains to do the impossible—make a high-rising bread. Instead, these grains were used in applications that well suited their nature. We would do well to take a cue from these traditions and not attempt to fit a buckwheat-shaped grain into a wheat-shaped hole.

That does not mean that sourdough loaves, buns and muffins cannot (or should not) be made using gluten-free grains. Read on and you'll find out how good these gluten-free breads really can be. It just means that the recipe needs a bit of help in getting there, in the form of additional ingredients that will mimic the work of the gluten protein.

I am happy to say that the flavor, texture and aroma of real sourdough bread can be had with gluten-free grains, and some of the recipes in this chapter are truly imperceptibly gluten-free. In fact, the fermentation process—and the acidity and depth of flavor it lends—makes for a much better gluten-free bread.

Gluten-Free Sourdough vs. Wheat Sourdough

When transitioning from wheat to gluten-free sourdough baking, there are both similarities and differences. Where there are similarities, you can take your knowledge of wheat baking and apply it to the gluten-free dough in front of you. But be aware of the differences lest you attempt to overcorrect a dough that is right on track.

Similarities include:

1. The arc of the sourdough process of mixing the dough, bulk fermentation, shaping and baking will remain. These steps may look slightly different, as the recipes will reflect, but generally the steps are all there.

2. Contrary to popular belief, kneading (for a stiff dough) or mixing (for a batter dough) are actually very necessary in making gluten-free sourdough breads. This step incorporates air into the dough, which the sourdough starter goes crazy for. This bit of aeration is critical not only for a good rise and great flavor, but also to make sure that all ingredients are truly incorporated and hydrated, in order to avoid the grittiness often found in gluten-free baked goods. You are not developing gluten, however, so a long kneading time is not necessary.

3. The feel of the dough, when ground psyllium husk is used, is very much akin to a high-hydration wheat dough. It is sticky and slightly wet but not so loose as to be considered a batter. You can then shape and knead this dough like you would a high-hydration wheat dough, though you will not want to add any additional flour during the process of kneading to avoid a heavy, dense loaf.

Differences include:

1. For starch-heavy grains such as rice (white and brown) and millet, both the sourdough starter and the recipes that utilize it will have a faster fermentation time. Starch is consumed quickly by the microbes in the sourdough starter, giving it a faster rise time. For that reason, I prefer sorghum or teff as the base of the gluten-free sourdough starter so the rise times are more akin to those made with a wheat sourdough starter.

2. If you are looking for something similar to what you can achieve with wheat bread, you'll need a few extra ingredients to mix into the dough, namely, binders of all sorts including ground psyllium husk, eggs and seeds such as flax and chia.

3. While large loaves such as the Gluten-Free Sourdough Seeded Country Loaf (page 107) are possible, individual breads such as English Muffins (page 103) or Dinner Rolls (page 104) lend themselves well to a lighter bread; the larger breads are simply too heavy to trap as much carbon dioxide as the smaller ones do.

On Gluten-Free Flour Choices

When you are baking gluten-free, it is easy to have a half-dozen or more flours on hand. Recipes often call for several different flours in order to get the correct ratio of starch to fiber to protein. This can be frustrating but, more often than not, if you want something akin to a wheat baked good, you really want to use more than one flour.

Having all of these flours on hand leads to the question: How do I substitute one flour for another? The answer is definitely not cut-and-dried and frankly, you need to expect variation in the final product when you make such a swap.

That said, at home I do swap flours in gluten-free baking based on what I have on hand. Here are my go-to swaps:

Rice Flours

Rice flour adds chewiness to bread like nothing else. Therefore, I generally only substitute brown rice flour for white rice flour and vice versa. Sweet rice flour is entirely different and, while it is considered a starch in baking, it does not substitute one-for-one with other starches with similar results.

Whole Grains

I really like to use whole-grain flours as much as possible, first, because it is similar to what we would grow and grind here on the homestead, and second, it is generally much less expensive to buy a bulk bag of organic millet or sorghum flour than it is to purchase all of the mixes or starches.

I use sorghum and teff flours interchangeably. Both have a nutty flavor and behave a lot like wheat in baked goods. I will also use buckwheat flour in place of these, if the application is conducive to the unique, bold flavor of buckwheat. Millet flour can also be used interchangeably with other flours, with the understanding that it tends to be a bit drier. For that reason, I would only substitute half the quantity of sorghum or teff with millet, and then replace the rest with rice or another whole-grain flour.

Starches

Starchy flours are often maligned in the world of gluten-free baking. The concern is that starches convert easily to sugar in the body, which can cause inflammation, blood sugar spikes and so forth. The other concern, which I share even in sourdough baking, is that they are simply very processed. For that reason, I tend to stick with two starches, both of which come from root vegetables.

Arrowroot and tapioca starches are my choice in gluten-free sourdough baking. I am not concerned with the possibility of high starch content, because the starch is actually helpful in sourdough baking and, much like wheat, the fermentation process metabolizes the starch ahead of time, converting it into a form that does not impact the body as unfermented starch might.

In replacing starches, arrowroot is generally a good exchange for potato and corn starches. Tapioca is in a category all its own, however, as it lends elasticity and a binding quality to breads that the other starches do not impart.

Gluten-Free Binders

The final element of gluten-free sourdough baking to consider is the binders necessary to create a bread that rises and has a similar crumb to wheat breads. Something needs to hold the dough together in order to re-create the elastic nature of gluten that traps carbon dioxide for a risen loaf.

The common binders used in gluten-free baking are xanthan gum and guar gum. I have worked with these, and they can create some surprisingly wheat-like breads. While they seemed to work, I wasn't sure where to buy a xanthan gum plant and, after a while, I wanted to branch out and see if I could create baked goods without them, instead using less-processed binders.

Xanthan gum is entirely man-made in a lab. It is incredibly processed and has no natural plant source. Although it is fermented, ironically, it was discovered when studying the use of a range of biopolymers. It was then introduced into the food system after being tested for safety on animals in 1968.

Guar gum comes from the guar bean, which, of course, has its origin in the guar tree. While it comes from a natural plant source, the process for manufacturing guar gum is extensive and involves both mechanical and chemical means. On a side note, 70 percent of guar gum products are used in manufacturing applications and the vast majority of those applications are directly involved in the fracking process.

With that in mind, the three binders I now prefer to use include:

Ground psyllium seed husk powder. It sounds a bit strange, but this is simply a portion of the seed from the *Plantago ovata* plant. This guy grows in western and southern Asia, and has even been introduced into the southwestern United States. A portion of the seed—the husk—is broken off and the resultant husk is used whole or is ground. The recipes in this book call for the latter type of psyllium husk.

Eggs. A common ingredient in most kitchens, pastured eggs impart a host of health benefits along with their ability to bind. Eggs lend elasticity, richness, flavor and protein to bread doughs and have long been used to enrich both wheat and gluten-free breads.

Mucilaginous seeds. When mixed with water, flax and chia seeds both have a mucilaginous (sticky) quality. This is helpful in gluten-free baking as it lends moisture and elasticity to breads.

Making Whole Wheat Breads with These Recipes

You can substitute up to 50 percent whole wheat flour for the white flour with little change to the end product. If you'd like to go 100 percent whole wheat, you'll need to alter the hydration slightly.

This isn't an exact science, but my protocol is to add ¼ cup (60 ml) of water for every 3½ cups (437 g) of flour when changing a recipe from all-purpose flour to whole wheat flour. Keep in mind that during the fermentation process, the bran will break down, resulting in a smoother dough over time. Intensive kneading just after mixing, therefore, is not as desirable as frequent stretching and folding, as in the 100% Whole Wheat Sourdough Sandwich Bread (page 91).

HOW TO MAKE A SOURDOUGH STARTER

Great bread, whether wheat or gluten-free, is made with simple ingredients, as is the sourdough starter from whence it is leavened. A simple slurry of flour and water come together to create a matrix for the bacteria, yeasts, enzymes and acids that will, quite literally, bring your bread to new heights.

Making a sourdough starter is a process, much like reaching the sweet spot for kimchi or kraut. I find that about a week, give or take, is all you need to create a sourdough starter that could last you a lifetime, if cared for properly. On the flipside, if all you want to do is a one-off sourdough bake, give yourself a week of daily starter care and you'll have the bread you were looking for.

A quick note on flour choice: Unbleached all-purpose flour, whole wheat flour, spelt flour and rye flour can all be used to make a starter for leavening wheat breads. Use the same guidelines for creating a gluten-free sourdough starter, but substitute teff, sorghum or buckwheat flour; other gluten-free flours are generally too starchy to create a good starter.

This week-long timeline will guide you through creating the gluten-free or wheat starter needed for baking.

Days One through Three: In a quart (1-L) jar, combine ½ cup (62 g) of flour and a scant ½ cup (118 ml) of water. Mix vigorously to incorporate air. Cover with a clean cloth, paper towel or coffee filter and secure with a rubber band or canning ring. Leave at room temperature (65 to 85°F [16 to 29°C]) for 12 hours. Repeat feedings with the same amounts of flour and water every 12 hours.

During this period, tiny bubbles may begin to form. The starter may start to smell really funky or just pleasantly sour. Either case is okay—simply forge ahead. By the third day, you may see a bit more yeast activity, indicated by bubbles and a larger volume of starter noticeable several hours after feeding.

Days Four through Seven: For a wheat sourdough starter, begin feeding every 24 hours and discard half of the starter before every feeding. For recipes that will use up that discarded starter, see page 81. For a gluten-free sourdough starter, continue to feed every 12 hours and discard half of the starter before every feeding.

You will now begin to see more yeast activity. Your starter may start to double in volume four to eight hours after feeding it. It should begin to take on yeast aromas in addition to the sour aroma it should already have. The microorganisms are beginning to find a balance between yeasts and bacteria, and we want to continue encouraging yeast growth by continuing to feed it on a daily basis. If it begins to show funky-colored molds on top, or if it smells really bad (think rotten vegetable matter), you'll want to throw it out and start over. This happens pretty rarely, but you'll know it when you see it.

At about the six- to seven-day mark, your starter should indicate signs of being ready to leaven breads. Look for active, bubbly, doubling starter with a pleasant sourdough aroma. At this point you can (and should!) bake with it, feed it again and then continue with the maintenance path of your choosing.

HOW TO MAINTAIN A SOURDOUGH STARTER: DAILY OR WEEKLY

Once your starter is fully active and usable in baking, it is time to determine whether you want to have sourdough starter on hand for baking any day of the week that you choose, or if you would prefer to go the lower-maintenance route and store it in the refrigerator for weekly baking.

Daily Maintenance

If you choose to keep a starter on hand to bake with at your leisure, you will need to continue the daily feedings as indicated. This takes literally two minutes every day and allows you to have starter on hand for pancakes, breads, crackers and more. For gluten-free starter, a twelve-hour feeding schedule is better, but missing a feeding here and there is generally okay.

Weekly Maintenance

The other option, if it is available to you, is to employ your refrigerator to store your starter. The cold storage halts the fermentation process so your starter is not "hungry" after 24 hours. In this scenario, you will need to remove your starter 24 hours before baking. Feed it twice before you are ready to bake, both to build up the quantity of the starter to the amount you'll need for baking and also to feed and aerate it to wake it up and get the yeasts and bacteria active again.

Pros and Cons of Each Strategy

Obviously, a daily maintenance schedule is more rigorous. Forgetting a feeding here and there won't kill your starter, but it may set it back enough that you'll need to give it frequent feedings and aerations again before you can bake bread with it.

On the other hand, if you are active in the kitchen and cook or bake regularly with grains, daily maintenance gives you active starter at your fingertips so you can create breads and treats or ferment whole grains and even make Sourdough Bread Kvass (see page 167).

In my experience, there is a downside to storing a sourdough starter in the refrigerator. Certain bacteria and yeasts thrive in a particular range of temperatures and acidities. Throwing a starter accustomed to room temperature into the refrigerator generally results in at least a subtle change in its flavor and activity. It generally still works well at leavening and fermenting bread, but it is different. Colder temperatures also tend to stress a starter out so if you frequently forget feedings *and* store your starter in the refrigerator, you may end up disappointed in its leavening ability and flavor.

ACTIVE STARTER: HOW TO USE YOUR STARTER AT ITS PEAK

The starter is the backbone of your bread; you will want to incorporate it into the dough when it is the most vigorous. It should not be stressed by a lack of food or large variance in temperature. It should be used toward the end of its feeding cycle, having doubled in volume and being ready to consume the starches in the flour to create carbon dioxide.

In practical terms, this starter has its convex meniscus at its peak in your jar. If, just after stirring in the flour and water of the previous feeding, your starter's volume was 2 cups (473 ml), the active starter will be nearly 4 cups (946 ml) and will be filled with visible air bubbles.

The Case for Thick Starters

Judging the activity of your starter is made easier by keeping it thick enough that air bubbles are visible through the jar. At the very least, your starter should be as thick as pancake batter. Gluten-free starters may, therefore, require you to adjust the amount of liquid down to achieve this viscosity. A slight adjustment in the starter hydration such as this is not sufficient enough to affect the outcome of the final product.

ABOUT THE RECIPES

To take hot bread from the oven and serve it up warm and buttery is an act of love and an honor to perform. To the one with celiac or the one with a busy schedule; to those with gluten sensitivity or those who want biscuits without baking powder—these recipes are for you.

Pull warm, long-fermented Sourdough Flour-Free Oatmeal Cookies (page 100) out of the oven and serve them to your children. Slice Sourdough Sandwich Bread (page 84) or Gluten-Free Seeded Sourdough Country Loaf (page 107) for your morning toast. Make Sourdough Biscuits (page 92) or Overnight Sourdough Pancakes (page 99) with no leavening other than that which is in the sourdough starter.

And if all you want is that Quintessential Sourdough Bread (page 88) you found when you lived by San Francisco Bay, try that loaf as well. I have tried and tested these recipes—some for several years now—in our off-grid kitchen, so they are easy to make with readily available ingredients.

The gluten-free recipes in this book are simple enough to make using whole-grain flours plus a bit of tapioca or arrowroot starch, with psyllium husk as a binder. There are no gums in these recipes. The Gluten-Free Sourdough English Muffins (page 103) were such a revelation to me that I had to hunt down my husband in the goat pasture and give him a taste. When eaten fresh, they are just good English muffins with no hint of being gluten-free.

And for those of us who love simplicity, I have shared our version of fermented staple foods—Porridge (with any grain, page 111) and Polenta (page 115) made from stone-ground cornmeal. There is truly something for every occasion and everyone in this chapter, which is just how bread ought to be—something we *all* can come together around.

Seven Ways to Use Discarded Starter

When you are regularly feeding your starter, you may have discarded starter to deal with. Just because it is referred to as discarded does not mean you can't use it. Give it a whirl in these baked goods:

Pancake batter. This is the simplest and most common use for excess starter. If you keep your starter on the thick side, just add an egg to 1½ cups (360 ml) of starter and then mix in a pinch of salt and ¼ teaspoon baking soda.

Crepes. Another simple solution is to mix 1 cup (237 ml) of sourdough starter with three eggs and a pinch of salt. Add milk to thin, if needed, and cook in a buttered pan.

Savory fritters. For something different, I like to mix 1 cup (237 ml) of sourdough starter, 1 egg and 1 cup (150 g) of finely chopped vegetables. Add salt, garlic, onion, ¼ cup (30 g) of cheese and herbs to taste, and fry in lard or coconut oil.

Beyond these three staples, you can:

1. Mix it into any quick bread batter

2. Use it as a culture starter for kvasses

3. Feed it to chickens or pigs

4. Throw it into the compost pile as a last resort

Wheat Sourdough English Muffins

The key to nooks and crannies, it turns out, is a wet dough that is handled very little. Air pockets remain when you don't punch it out; an open crumb is possible when little kneading is involved and the dough's hydration is high. Working with the dough and getting the cooking temperature just right are the trickiest part of this recipe, but once you get the feel for it, you won't believe how simple these guys are to make.

Ferment them overnight for warm muffins first thing in the morning. Or, if you know you'll be rushed for time, let them ferment all day, bake them at night and toast them up for breakfast the next morning.

 Makes: 12 to 16 muffins / Fermentation Time: 8 to 12 hours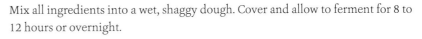

4 cups (500 g) flour

1 tbsp (15 g) salt

1 cup (237 ml) sourdough starter (page 79)

2 tbsp (30 ml) honey

1½ cups (355 ml) plus 2 tbsp (30 ml) water

Organic cornmeal or additional flour as needed

Mix all ingredients into a wet, shaggy dough. Cover and allow to ferment for 8 to 12 hours or overnight.

Generously flour a clean work surface or sprinkle generously with cornmeal. Turn the dough out onto the work surface and generously flour or sprinkle with cornmeal. Pat the dough out into a ¾-inch (19-mm) thick rectangle, being careful to make it as even as possible.

Cover the dough lightly with a damp towel or plastic wrap and allow to rise for 30 minutes to 1 hour.

Preheat a griddle or large skillet over medium-low heat. Cut the English muffins from the dough using a round 3-inch (75-mm) biscuit cutter or, to avoid any waste, cut into 2½-inch (64-mm) squares using a large knife or bench scraper.

Once the griddle is hot, carefully transfer English muffins to griddle as they are, with the bottoms down. They will be wobbly and slightly difficult to work with, so just transfer them as best as you can, leaving ½ to 1 inch (13 to 25 mm) between each muffin.

Bake for 4 to 7 minutes on the first side, or until golden brown on the bottom and puffed up slightly on top. Gently flip the muffins by picking them up with a spatula, grabbing ahold of the bottom portion of the sides with your fingers, and turning them over. If the muffin seems uneven, simply give it a little press to even it out. Allow to cook an additional 4 to 7 minutes, or until golden brown. If they brown faster than you expect, turn the heat down slightly and flip the muffins more than once for even cooking without burning. They will get a bit dark but shouldn't burn.

Transfer to a wire rack to cool. To split, poke the sides of the muffin with a fork all the way around and then split it open with the fork. Toast or eat as is with butter or jam, or stuffed with eggs.

Wheat Sourdough Sandwich Bread

This bread is a good example of utilizing a sticky dough, and almost no kneading, to achieve that fluffy, soft, quintessential sandwich bread texture. With a slight tang and a moist crumb, this bread holds up well to slicing, toasting or lunch box sandwiches.

Makes: 1 loaf / Fermentation Time: 10 to 12 hours

1 cup (237 ml) sourdough starter (page 79)

3 tbsp (45 ml) honey

1½ cups (355 ml) milk

2 eggs

3 tbsp (45 ml) olive oil

2 tsp (10 g) salt

3 cups (375 g) flour

Combine all of the liquid ingredients and whisk well. Add the salt and flour and mix until a sticky, shaggy dough comes together. Once all of the ingredients are well incorporated and the flour is hydrated, cover the bowl and leave to ferment for approximately 4 hours.

Uncover the bowl and lightly flour your hands and the surface of the dough. Turn the dough over onto itself by pulling up from the bottom of the dough and stretching it over the top and onto the opposite side. Repeat 3 to 4 times, moving around the perimeter of the dough. Recover the dough and allow to rest for an additional 4 to 5 hours.

Generously grease a 9 x 5-inch (23 x 13-cm) bread pan, being careful to also grease the top rim of the pan. Lightly flour a clean work surface and turn the dough out onto it. Lightly flour the surface of the dough and pat it out into a rectangle. Roll the dough into a loaf shape, starting at one of the shorter ends of the rectangle. The dough will still be quite loose so pinch the seam closed as best as you can and transfer it to the greased bread pan.

Oil the surface of the dough and cover with plastic wrap or a slightly dampened towel. Leave to rise for 2 to 4 hours, depending on the temperature, or until the peak of the dough has risen to 1 inch (25 mm) above the rim of the pan. Once the dough has reached the rim of the pan, preheat the oven to 375°F (190°C).

Once the dough has fully risen to 1 inch (25 mm) above the rim of the pan, gently slash the top of the loaf with a very sharp knife. Place the pan in the preheated oven and bake for 35 to 40 minutes or until an internal temperature of 180°F (82°C) has been reached.

Remove to a cooling rack and allow to cool for at least 1 hour before slicing.

Wheat Sourdough Crescent Rolls

These are the dinner rolls of your dreams. Rich, sweet and pillowy soft, they taste like the dinner rolls you pass around at every celebration meal. Except for the fact that these are fermented for a good 8 hours, require no kneading and taste like a dream when baked with 100 percent whole wheat flour.

Makes: 16 rolls / Fermentation Time: 8 hours

4 cups (500 g) flour

2½ tsp (13 g) salt

2 eggs

¾ cup (177 ml) sourdough starter (page 79)

⅓ cup (80 ml) honey

1 cup (237 ml) milk

½ cup (115 g) softened butter

Combine the flour and salt in a large mixing bowl. Form a well in the middle of the flour and crack and whisk the eggs in. Add the starter, honey, milk and softened butter. Mix all ingredients well with a wooden spoon until a thick, sticky dough is formed. Scrape down the sides of the bowl and gather all of the dough into the center.

Cover the bowl and allow to rest for 8 hours (all day or overnight) at room temperature.

Divide the dough in half. Generously flour a work surface. Scrape one half of the dough out onto the work surface. Dust the surface of the dough with flour and gently roll it out into a ⅛-inch (3-mm)-thick circle. Using a pizza cutter, cut the dough into 8 triangles.

Working from the widest point of each triangle, roll the dough to the tip, forming a crescent roll shape. Move each crescent roll to a well-greased or parchment-lined sheet pan. Repeat with other half of the dough.

Cover the pan of crescent rolls and allow to rise for 1 hour. Preheat the oven to 375°F (190°C). Bake the rolls for 15 to 20 minutes or until browned on the bottom and just becoming golden on top. Allow to cool for at least 10 minutes before serving.

Quintessential Sourdough Farm Loaf

With flour, salt, starter and water, this bread is an everyday loaf for serving with soups, dunking in olive oil or toasting for breakfast. It is chewy, light and tangy—all that you look for in a loaf of sourdough bread. You can enrich it with honey and butter, but whatever you do, try not to add much flour when kneading. I learned this broken-up kneading technique from the great Peter Reinhart, and it really works to avoid a dense, heavy bread brought on by too much flour.

 Makes: 2 average round loaves / Fermentation Time: 8 to 12 hours

5½ cups (687 g) flour

2½ tsp (13 g) sea salt

1 cup (237 ml) sourdough starter (page 79)

1½ cups (355 ml) water

3 tbsp (45 ml) honey (optional)

3 tbsp (43 g) softened butter (optional)

Combine the flour and salt in a large mixing bowl. Make a well in the middle of the flour and add the starter, water, honey and softened butter if using. Mix all ingredients well with a wooden spoon until a rough dough begins to form.

Knead the dough in the bowl for a couple of minutes. It will be shaggy and sticky at this stage. Let the dough rest for 5 minutes. Return to the dough and knead it for 3 minutes. Let the dough rest for 2 more minutes and then give it a final 1- to 2-minute knead until smooth and soft.

Cover the bowl tightly and allow the dough to ferment for 8 to 12 hours or overnight.

When ready to bake, uncover the bread and grease a large baking pan. Divide the dough in half and shape it into a round boule or a long batard. Place on the greased baking sheet, leaving a couple of inches between the loaves. Sprinkle the surface of the loaves with flour and cover with plastic wrap or a damp towel to rise. Leave for 1 to 2 hours until risen by 50 to 75 percent.

During the last 30 minutes of rise time, preheat the oven to 400°F (204°C). Once the oven is hot and the dough has risen substantially, uncover. Give the dough a few slashes with a razor or very sharp knife. Place the loaves in the hot oven and bake for 35 to 40 minutes or until the bottom sounds hollow when tapped and the internal temperature has reached 190°F (88°C).

Move to a cooling rack and allow to cool for at least 20 minutes before serving.

100% Whole Wheat Sourdough Sandwich Bread

This is an all-day bread, in that you begin it first thing in the morning and bake it last thing at night. If, like me, you like to have a timeline instead of a recipe, it looks like this: 8:00 a.m.: Mix dough; 11:00 a.m.: Stretch and fold; 2:00 p.m.: Stretch and fold; 4:00 p.m.: Stretch and fold; 6:00 p.m.: Shape and rise; 8:00 to 9:00 p.m.: Bake.

 Makes: One 9 x 5-inch (23 x 13-cm) loaf / Fermentation Time: 12 to 14 hours

3½ cups (455 g) whole wheat flour

1⅓ cups (308 ml) milk or water

2 tsp (10 g) salt

½ cup (118 ml) sourdough starter (page 79)

2 tbsp (30 ml) honey

2 tbsp (30 ml) melted coconut oil or butter

First thing in the morning, combine all of the ingredients in a medium bowl and mix well with a fork or wooden spoon until all of the flour has been hydrated. At this point, the dough will be very rough and shaggy.

Cover the bowl and leave to rest in a warm spot in your kitchen for approximately 3 hours. After this initial time period, you may or may not notice that the dough has puffed up. We're not looking for any doubling in volume; we are simply working the dough quickly and gently to develop the gluten.

Uncover the dough, which will be sticky, and in the bowl, stretch and fold it upon itself 4 or 5 times. It helps to see the dough as a clock. To do this, simply grab the 12 o'clock spot on your dough, and fold it into the center of the ball. Move from 12 o'clock to 3 o'clock and so on until the dough has stretched upon itself from every direction. A final folding can be done to neaten up the ball of dough. Flip the dough over. After this first stretch-and-fold, the dough will appear a lot smoother than before. Cover the bowl again and leave for an additional 2 to 3 hours.

Repeat the stretch-and-fold technique. Let the dough rest 2 to 3 more hours and repeat one final time. The beauty of this recipe is that none of these time spans have to be exact and you do not have to wait for the dough to double in between, though it will rise a bit. Two to three hours before you wish to be done in the kitchen for the day, shape the loaf for the final rise. (Two hours in warmer weather, three in cooler.) To do this, either grease a 9 × 5-inch (23 x 13-cm) glass bread pan or a baking sheet with butter or another solid fat or grease. Shape into a loaf or a round boule by tucking the dough under and forming a ball. When shaping a boule, try to make the ball higher than it is wide, because it can spread a bit during the rise period.

Once shaped, leave the dough to rise for 1 to 2 hours, or until it has risen by approximately 75 percent. Preheat the oven to 375°F (190°C) during the last 30 minutes of rise time.

Bake the bread in the middle of the preheated oven for 25 to 32 minutes, or until it reaches an internal temperature of 200°F (93°C) or sounds hollow when the bottom of the loaf is thumped. Transfer to a cooling rack and allow to cool completely before slicing.

Sourdough Biscuits
Sans Baking Powder or Soda

Biscuits can be made without baking powder or baking soda, I hypothesized. These biscuits are light and the texture is somewhere between a baking powder biscuit and a dinner roll. They are truly delicious.

 Makes: 10 to 12 biscuits / Fermentation Time: 6 to 10 hours

2 cups (250 g) flour plus more for forming

1½ tsp (8 g) sea salt

⅓ cup (76 g) cold lard, butter or palm shortening

1¼ cups (296 ml) sourdough starter (page 79)

¼–½ cup (59–118 ml) milk

1 egg, beaten with 1 tbsp (15 ml) water

Combine the flour and salt with a fork. Cut the lard, butter or shortening into the flour mixture until the fat is the size of small peas. Add the sourdough starter and milk, starting with ¼ cup (60 ml) of milk. If, as you are mixing, it looks as though the dough may be too stiff, add more milk until a sticky but cohesive dough is formed. Stir only until all of the ingredients have come together.

Cover and allow to rest for 1 to 2 hours at room temperature.

Prepare a 12-inch (30-cm) cast-iron skillet or two 9-inch (23-cm) pie pans by generously greasing and sprinkling the bottom with flour. Have additional flour ready for use in forming the biscuits. Dip one hand in flour and, using a large spoon, scoop approximately 2 tablespoons (23 g) of the dough from the bowl. Shape the dough roughly into a round using the floured hand and place it in the prepared skillet. Repeat with the remaining biscuits, spacing them approximately ¼ inch (6 mm) apart. You can form 10 large biscuits or 12 smaller ones.

Set aside to rise for 4 to 8 hours or until doubled in size. Brush tops with egg wash. Bake at 400°F (204°C) for 30 to 35 minutes, or until golden brown underneath.

Multipurpose Wheat Sourdough Tortillas or Flatbreads

This dough can be used to roll out large, thin tortillas or chewy, naan-style flatbreads. I like to start fermenting the tortillas in the morning for a taco night or just before bed for breakfast burritos or lunch the next day. The hard part for me is rolling that elusive perfect circle of a tortilla. Once on the hot griddle, however, all is forgotten as I watch them steam and puff up. Do use milk, if you can, as it lends tenderness to the tortillas.

 Makes: 12 to 16 tortillas or 12 flatbreads / Fermentation Time: 8 to 12 hours

3½ cups (375 g) flour, plus more for rolling

2 tsp (10 g) salt

½ cup (110 g) lard, coconut oil or butter

1 cup (237 ml) milk or water

1 cup (237 ml) sourdough starter (page 79)

Mix the flour and salt together with a fork. Cut the fat into the flour mixture until it is the size of peas. Add the milk or water and sourdough starter. Mix all ingredients well until a shaggy dough comes together. Cover the bowl tightly.

Allow to ferment for 8 to 12 hours—all day for an evening meal or overnight for breakfast or lunch. Uncover the dough and preheat a griddle or large skillet over medium-high heat.

Divide the dough into 12 equal pieces for large tortillas or naan-style flatbreads or 16 for smaller tortillas. Roll each piece of dough into a ball and place into the bowl, and cover with a damp towel.

Flour a clean work surface and a rolling pin. Place one of the dough balls on the floured work surface and roll into desired shape. Roll tortillas into circles as thin as possible without breaking; roll naan breads into ⅛-inch (3-mm)-thick ovals.

Carefully transfer one tortilla or naan bread to the hot griddle and allow to cook for 2 minutes. Flip and cook 2 to 3 minutes. Transfer the tortilla or naan bread to a towel-lined basket. Repeat with remaining dough, covering the cooked tortillas or naan bread with the towel between each addition.

Serve warm or store cooled leftovers in an airtight container. Warm gently on a griddle to reheat, sprinkling with a bit of water as they warm to keep them moist.

Seasonal Fruit Fermented Muffins

Just sweet enough and studded with the season's freshest fruits, these sourdough muffins have won a place in our breakfast hearts. Texas peaches come in buckets around here, and while sticky fingers and chins are our constant companions, recipes like this use up what remains. This isn't technically a sourdough recipe, though you can use sourdough starter to ferment the batter. Because of the addition of baking powder and baking soda, kombucha and milk kefir are also great candidates for the fermentation liquid. Feel free to halve this recipe in case your family can't devour 24 muffins in 48 hours like mine can.

 Makes: 2 dozen muffins / Fermentation Time: 8 to 24 hours

4 cups (500 g) all-purpose flour

1 ¾ cups (427 ml) milk

¼ cup (61 ml) kombucha, milk kefir or sourdough starter

3 eggs, beaten

½ cup (118 ml) melted butter, cooled

½ tsp sea salt

½ cup (96 g) granulated sweetener (sucanat, sugar, coconut sugar)

2 tsp (10 ml) vanilla extract (optional)

1 tbsp (11 g) baking powder

½ tsp baking soda

2 cups (360 g) chopped fresh peaches or other fresh fruit

In a medium mixing bowl, combine the flour, milk and fermentation liquid of choice just until the flour is mostly hydrated. A few lumps here and there are okay. Cover tightly and allow to ferment for 8 to 24 hours, keeping in mind that the shorter the fermentation time, the less sour the end product will be.

When ready to bake, grease or line two 12-cup muffin tins and preheat the oven to 400°F (204°C). Uncover the fermented dough and add the eggs, butter and salt to the bowl along with the sugar, vanilla or any other flavorings or spices you wish to add. Stir a few strokes to begin combining. At this point, the batter will be stretchy and a bit tough.

Sprinkle the baking powder and baking soda over the batter and combine with a wooden spoon or, if you are like me, you may prefer to use clean hands, as the batter is a bit hard to mix. Just before the batter is completely mixed, fold in the peaches or fresh fruit of your choosing. Mix the batter only as much as is needed to combine the ingredients.

Divide the dough among the 24 muffins cups and place the pans in the preheated oven. Bake for 20 to 25 minutes or until the tops have turned golden brown and a toothpick comes out clean when inserted into the middle of the muffin.

Transfer to a cooling rack and allow to cool for 10 to 15 minutes before serving with butter.

Overnight Wheat Sourdough Pancakes Sans Baking Powder or Soda

Have you ever wanted to wake up to a fully-prepared bowl of pancake batter and simply ladle it onto the hot griddle while you sip your first cup of coffee? Getting one step ahead of breakfast is imperative in my home, and this recipe gets the job done with these thick, tangy and sweet little guys. They are not the big, round fluffy pancakes from the diner, but they are a delicious cross between a traditional pancake and a sweet roll, and they stun with syrup, butter and a side of pastured pork sausage.

 Makes: 16 to 20 small pancakes / Fermentation Time: 8 to 12 hours, or overnight

2 eggs, beaten

1¼ cups (296 ml) milk

1 cup (237 ml) sourdough starter (page 79)

¼ cup (60 ml) honey

2 tsp (10 ml) vanilla extract

4 tbsp (60 ml) melted butter, cooled

2 cups (250 g) flour (all-purpose or pastry)

1 tsp (5 g) salt

In a large bowl, beat the eggs, milk, starter, honey, vanilla and butter together until homogenous.

Add the flour and salt, and mix just until all ingredients are moistened and mostly combined. A few lumps are okay.

Cover the bowl tightly with a lid and leave to ferment overnight. If you are leery of leaving eggs and milk overnight on the counter, simply transfer the bowl to the refrigerator overnight. In the morning, remove the bowl from the refrigerator 30 minutes before you plan to cook the pancakes.

Preheat a large griddle or skillet over medium heat and lightly grease its surface. Scoop ¼ cup (60 ml) of pancake batter onto the griddle to form a small pancake. Repeat with as many as will fit in your pan, leaving at least ¼ inch (6 mm) of space between the pancakes. Cook the pancakes for 3 to 4 minutes on the first side, or until golden brown. Carefully flip and cook the second side for an additional 3 to 4 minutes.

Because these take longer to cook, it is a good idea to test a pancake before removing the whole lot from the pan. Simply cut into the middle of one pancakes on the griddle to ensure that it has cooked all the way through. If it is done, move to a platter and serve. If not, continue cooking for 4 more minutes, flipping the cakes again as needed to prevent burning.

Finish cooking remaining batter. Serve warm with your favorite toppings.

Sourdough Flour-Free Oatmeal Cookies

After years of my attempts to make a sourdough cookie that actually tastes like a cookie—not a cake—my husband was thrilled when these came out of the oven. Freshly baked, they are crispy around the edges and soft in the middle; once cooled, they are chewy and sweet with just enough tang and salt to make them irresistible. Make them gluten-free with a gluten-free sourdough starter and certified GF oats.

 Makes: 16 to 20 small cookies / Fermentation Time: 8 to 24 hours

¼ cup (55 g) butter or shortening

½ cup (196 g) unrefined sugar such as sucanat or coconut

2 cups (161 g) quick cooking oats (gluten-free if desired)

¾ cup (177 ml) sourdough starter (page 79)

2 tbsp (19 g) ground flaxseed

1 tsp (3 g) cinnamon

¾ tsp fine-grained sea salt

¼ tsp baking soda

½ cup (75 g) raisins, optional

2 tsp (10 ml) vanilla extract

Cream the butter or shortening with the sugar. Add the oats, starter and flaxseed meal and stir to combine. Knead until dough just comes together. Cover tightly and allow to ferment at room temperature for 8 to 24 hours, as desired.

When ready to bake, preheat the oven to 350°F (177°C) and prepare a cookie sheet by lightly greasing or lining it with parchment paper.

Uncover the fermented oat mixture and break it up a bit with a fork. Use a fork to mix the cinnamon, salt, baking soda and raisins in a small bowl. Sprinkle this mixture over the dough and then drizzle the vanilla over the top. Knead all ingredients together with clean hands until the dough is homogenous.

Scoop approximately 2 tablespoons (23 g) of dough for each cookie. Place on the cookie sheet and flatten slightly with the back of a fork. Fill the cookie sheet, leaving a half inch (13 mm) of space between the cookies.

Place the baking sheet in the oven and bake for 15 to 20 minutes or until golden brown on bottom and around the edges and set completely in the middle.

Allow to cool for 5 minutes before transferring to a cooling rack.

Gluten-Free Sourdough English Muffins

The first time I made this recipe, it was a complete shot in the dark. I guessed at the flour combinations and theorized that it would work on a griddle as an English muffin. Ninety-five percent of the time these ideas flop. This was part of the 5 percent where I ran outside and made someone—anyone—taste this gluten-free bread which, fresh from the griddle, could easily be mistaken for wheat. There were nooks and crannies. There was a tender crumb and a crispy crust. Best of all, after finagling muffin rings and wet doughs and turning out hockey pucks from stiff doughs, this recipe is the easiest method I've tried for gluten-free English muffins.

 Makes: 12 to 16 muffins / Fermentation Time: 7 to 13 hours

1 cup (120 g) millet flour

1 cup (150 g) rice flour

1 cup (125 g) tapioca flour

2 tbsp (24 g) sugar

1½ tbsp (12 g) psyllium husk powder

2 tsp (10 g) sea salt

2 tbsp (29 g) softened butter

1¼ cups (296 ml) water

¾ cup (177 ml) sourdough starter (page 79)

TO FINISH

1 tsp (4 g) baking soda

¼ cup (59 ml) water

Combine all ingredients in a large mixing bowl. Beat with a wooden spoon for 2 to 3 minutes or until it becomes similar to a tacky bread dough. Cover tightly and let rise for 6 to 12 hours, or overnight. It will only have risen by about 50 percent.

In a small bowl, dissolve the baking soda in the water. Uncover the fermented dough and pour the baking soda mixture over the top. Combine the baking soda mixture with the fermented dough by working the dough and liquid between your fingers until the liquid has been absorbed and the baking soda is evenly dispersed. Be careful not to overmix, however.

Cover and let rise 1 hour.

Preheat a large griddle or cast-iron skillet over low heat. Once hot, lightly grease the pan. Remove approximately ¼ cup (60 ml) of dough and, with your hands, shape it into a circle roughly three-fourths of an inch (19 mm) tall. Place on the greased pan and continue with remaining dough, leaving at least 1 inch (25 mm) of space between the muffins.

Cook for 4 to 7 minutes on the first side or just until the bottoms become a deep golden brown and the edges are dry and set. Carefully flip and cook an additional 4 to 6 minutes or until the second side is golden brown.

Move cooked muffins to a cooling rack and allow to cool for at least 5 minutes before serving. To open, poke the sides of the English muffin with a fork all the way around the circumference and then pry it open. Toast if desired or eat warm with butter and jam.

Gluten-Free Sourdough Dinner Rolls

Rich in flavor, light in texture; chewy, sweet and soft. These are dinner rolls at their finest, and they also happen to be fermented and gluten-free.

 Makes: 12 rolls / Fermentation Time: 8 to 10 hours

2 eggs

1 cup (237 ml) milk

½ cup (118 ml) water

¼ cup (57 ml) melted butter or coconut oil, cooled

⅓ cup (78 ml) honey

½ cup (118 ml) gluten-free sourdough starter (page 79)

1 cup (151 g) rice flour

1¼ cups (150 g) millet flour

1 cup (125 g) tapioca flour

2½ tbsp (20 g) ground psyllium husk

2 tsp (10 g) salt

2 tbsp (16 g) ground flaxseed

Combine the eggs, milk, water, melted fat, honey and sourdough starter in a medium bowl. In a separate bowl, whisk together the flours, psyllium husk, salt and ground flaxseed. Add the flour mixture to the liquid mixture and mix together until combined. Using a wooden spoon or the paddle attachment of an electric mixer, beat the dough for an additional 5 minutes to strengthen the dough and incorporate air.

Cover and allow to ferment at room temperature for 6 to 8 hours or overnight. At this point, the dough will have risen by approximately 50 percent.

Two hours before you wish to bake and serve the rolls, uncover the fermented dough. Working carefully so as to not deflate the dough too much, divide it into 12 pieces. Gently form each piece of dough into a rounded dinner roll shape. Cover with plastic wrap or a lightly dampened towel and allow to rise for 2 hours, at which point the rolls will have puffed up slightly. Preheat the oven to 375°F (190°C).

Once the oven is hot, uncover the rolls and place them in the hot oven. Bake for 20 to 25 minutes or until golden and cooked through. Transfer to a basket and serve warm.

Gluten-Free Sourdough Seeded Country Loaf

This recipe is wholesome and simple enough to be your daily bread. After an overnight bulk ferment, it gets a couple of hours before being baked. My favorite part of this loaf is its keeping quality and how well it slices up for toast.

 Makes: One large loaf / Fermentation Time: 9½ to 14 hours

1¾ cups (414 ml) water

¾ cup (177 ml) gluten-free sourdough starter (page 79)

2 tbsp (30 ml) honey

2 tbsp (30 ml) oil

3 tbsp (24 g) ground flaxseed

2½ tbsp (20 g) ground psyllium husk

2 tbsp (16 g) chia seeds

1 cup (120 g) teff flour

¾ cup (94 g) tapioca flour

½ cup (64 g) sorghum flour

½ cup (60 g) millet flour

2 tsp (10 g) sea salt

In a large mixing bowl, whisk together the water, starter, honey and oil. In a separate bowl, whisk together all dry ingredients. Add the dry ingredients to the wet ones and mix with a wooden spoon or clean hands for approximately 3 minutes. At this point, the dough will still be quite moist.

Cover and allow to bulk ferment for 8 to 12 hours or overnight.

Grease a baking sheet and uncover the dough. Knead the dough a few times and shape it into a large boule. Place on the prepared baking sheet and cover lightly with a damp towel. Allow to rise 1½ to 2 hours, until puffed up slightly. During the last half hour of rise time, preheat the oven to 400°F (204°C).

Once it is risen, place the bread in the oven and bake for 55 to 65 minutes or until the internal temperature reaches 190°F (88°C). Allow to cool for 5 minutes before moving to a cooling rack. Let the loaf cool completely before slicing.

Gluten-Free Fluffy Sourdough Pancakes

A great piece of gluten-free baking advice I once received is to add an extra egg. This is particularly true for quick bread recipes like muffins and pancakes. These pancakes are robust with tangy buckwheat flavor while being fluffy and delicious. Raspberry jam is the perfect topping for these big pancakes, and I think adding butter goes without saying.

Makes: Pancakes for 4 to 6 / Fermentation Time: Overnight

½ cup (118 ml) gluten-free sourdough starter (page 79)

1 cup (170 g) buckwheat flour

⅔ cup (100 g) rice flour

1¼ cups (296 ml) milk

3 eggs

1 tsp (5 ml) vanilla extract

½ tsp salt

1 tbsp (11 g) baking powder

Combine the sourdough starter, buckwheat flour, rice flour and milk in a medium mixing bowl. Combine with a fork until all ingredients are hydrated. Cover and allow to ferment overnight at room temperature.

In the morning, preheat a griddle pan or skillet over medium heat. Uncover the fermented batter and mix lightly with a fork to break it up a bit. Make a well in the middle. Crack the eggs into the well and beat. Add the vanilla and salt and begin incorporating the egg mixture into the surrounding batter. Once the dough is nearly mixed, sprinkle the baking powder over the top and stir until completely combined.

When the griddle is hot, grease it lightly with butter, lard or coconut oil. Ladle ⅓ cup (80 ml) of the batter onto the griddle to form a pancake. Cook 2 to 3 minutes until small bubbles just begin to appear and the edges begin to firm. Carefully flip and cook an additional 2 to 3 minutes or until golden brown.

Serve piping hot with butter and jam, syrup or honey.

Perpetual Fermented Porridge

I am a strong believer in porridge for its history of nourishment and its simplicity in my kitchen. By keeping a porridge ferment going at all times, we can have a bowl when we want it without much forethought. This is especially helpful in winter when little hands cup warm bowls while cozying up to the big cast-iron wood stove. My favorite way to serve this is with grass-fed butter and maple syrup or raw honey. Tangy porridge is tasty porridge.

 Makes: 4 to 6 servings / Fermentation Time: 12 to 48 hours initially; 12 to 18 hours thereafter

2 cups (322 g) steel-cut oats or other whole or cracked grain, plus more as needed

Water, as needed

1 tbsp (15 ml) sourdough starter (page 79), water kefir or milk kefir whey (optional)

Add the oats to a half-gallon (2-L) jar and cover with enough water to fill to the 4-cup (1-L) measure. Add the sourdough starter, if using. Stir briskly with a wooden spoon and cover with a permeable lid such as a coffee filter or clean cloth. Secure the lid with a rubber band or canning ring.

Place the oats at warm room temperature and allow to ferment for 12 to 48 hours, checking for signs of fermentation starting at the 12-hour mark. Look for bubbles and a tangy aroma. Expect the fermentation time to take longer if you have not inoculated the oats with a culture starter.

Once the mixture begins to bubble and ferment, it is ready to use. Remove as much fermented mash as you would like, but be sure to leave at least a tablespoon (12 g) in the jar to inoculate the next batch. To perpetuate the next round of porridge, add in 2 more cups (322 g) of grain and cover with water as before. After the initial fermentation has been completed, the porridge should ferment within 12 to 18 hours. Continue harvesting, leaving a bit and feeding as needed for continual fermented porridge.

The porridge can be eaten raw and fermented as is, though if you have any digestive issues, you may have trouble digesting it in its raw state. For cooked porridge, simply add the fermented porridge and approximately half as much, in volume, of fresh water or milk to a small pot. So, if you are adding 3 cups (710 ml) of fermented porridge, add in 1½ cups (355 ml) of water.

Cook over a low heat until the grains are tender and the porridge is the consistency you desire, stirring often. Serve with cream, butter, coconut milk and your favorite sweeteners or toppings.

Sourdough Skillet Cornbread

That crisp-bottomed golden loaf can only be had with a hot oven and a cast-iron skillet. While I grew up eating the sweeter Northern cornbread, which generally contains more wheat flour and sugar, this recipe is much more akin to a Southern cornbread. Made only with cornmeal and fermented overnight with sourdough starter, this bread is all about the corn. The fermentation only improves the flavor and texture and makes it easier on the belly.

 Makes: 8 to 12 slices / Fermentation Time: 8 to 24 hours

1 cup (237 ml) sourdough starter (page 79)

2 cups (341 g) whole grain cornmeal

2 cups (474 ml) milk

3 eggs, beaten

2 tbsp (30 ml) honey

2 tbsp (30 ml) melted butter (or bacon grease)

2 tsp (8 g) baking powder

½ tsp baking soda

1 tsp (5 g) salt

At least 8 hours before you wish to bake and serve the cornbread, combine the starter, cornmeal and milk in a medium mixing bowl. Cover and allow to ferment 8 to 24 hours.

After the fermentation period is through, preheat your oven to 450°F (232°C). Grease a 12-inch (30-cm) cast-iron skillet and place it in the oven to preheat while you mix together the dough.

Whisk the eggs, honey and melted butter in a small bowl and add them to the fermented dough. Whisk until nearly combined. In another small bowl, mix together the baking powder, baking soda and salt with a fork. Sprinkle this mixture over the dough and quickly stir it in until completely combined. Immediately pour the batter into the skillet and place it in the oven.

Bake 20 to 25 minutes or until a knife or toothpick comes out clean when inserted into center of the bread. Allow to cool before cutting. Serve with butter and honey, or dunk into a hearty chili.

Fermented Polenta/Grits

The grits of the South are not unlike the polenta of Italy, which is not unlike a food termed "cornmeal mush." Besides cornbread, grits were one of the staple foods in the South when wheat was not readily had. Fermenting, either wild or with an added culture, and then cooking low and slow produces some really good, simple food. Note that fermenting corn is not the same process as nixtamalization, which utilizes calcium hydroxide–an alkaline solution– to process the corn into nixtamal for making tamales and corn tortillas.

 Makes: 4 to 6 cups (1 to 1.5 L) / Fermentation Time: 2 to 3 days

1 cup (170 g) coarse cornmeal

3 cups (710 ml) filtered water

2 tbsp (30 ml) sourdough starter or other culture starter (see page 79), optional

1-2 cups (237-473 ml) water, bone broth or milk, for cooking

1 tsp (5 g) sea salt

Combine the cornmeal and filtered water in a quart (1-L) jar. Add the culture starter, if using, and stir to combine. If doing a wild fermentation, cover the jar with a permeable lid secured with a canning ring or rubber band. If using a culture starter, place a lid loosely on the jar.

Leave jar to ferment for 2 to 3 days or until signs of fermentation begin–bubbling, a tangy smell and so forth.

Once fermented, cook the grits by mixing the fermented cornmeal with the water, broth or milk in a medium saucepan. Place over medium heat and bring to a boil. Turn the heat to low and simmer for 25 to 30 minutes, stirring frequently, until the cornmeal is the desired thickness. It will thicken upon cooling.

Dairy

It has been said that one of the most prized possessions for a pioneer family on the frontier was the family milk cow. With no refrigeration, no grocery store and no guarantee that the next hunt would bring some much-needed protein, this animal was an invaluable part of frontier life.

Now that we've started our own small herd of dairy animals—goats, to be exact—they have become a prized possession on our homestead and to date have produced the most homegrown calories of any of our agrarian endeavors.

The family milk animal produces food on a daily basis. Like most animals, it can forage on land that might otherwise not be suitable for human food production. The daily milking takes little time, bookending the day with animal chores. Best of all, it produces one of the most versatile, nutrient-dense foods a homesteader could hope for.

Milk can be drunk fresh, or skimmed and churned into butter. It can become a simple fermented food by incorporating a culture starter such as yogurt or milk kefir grains. It can be allowed to ferment naturally with a little exposure to oxygen for a thick, cultured dairy product. These fermented dairy products then have a longer shelf life than fresh milk, due to their acidic nature and imparted beneficial bacteria.

Clabber (a type of wild fermented milk), yogurt and kefir can all be drained to make a soft cheese with no need for rennet or further cultures. These cultured dairy products can be made into dips, salad dressings, fruit salads, breakfast bowls or smoothies, or stirred into main dishes to lend creaminess and staying power. Simple cheeses, fresh or aged, can also be made as a way of preserving the milk while providing the family with one more delicious way to consume the homegrown milk.

On top of all that, cultured dairy products are some of the most nutrient-dense foods you can consume. Assuming your animals are able to forage for a good part of their diet, the milk itself contains a good deal of vitamins and minerals often lacking in the plant food kingdom. Fermentation improves the vitamin content, breaks down hard-to-digest proteins and eliminates a good deal of the milk sugar known as lactose. All of that adds up to a vitamin- and mineral-rich food teeming with beneficial organisms, healthy fats and a good dose of quality protein.

HOW DAIRY FERMENTATION WORKS

When jars of fresh, unpasteurized milk are left on the counter, they begin to ferment. Naturally present bacteria go to work as soon as the necessary environmental boxes are checked off, and not long after that, spontaneous fermentation turns sweet liquid milk into something that tastes sour due to its lactic acid content. Note that this is only the case for raw milk. Pasteurized milk loses its inherent bacteria through the heating process, so it must be cultured through inoculation from outside bacteria.

Biologically speaking, dairy fermentation works much like grain and vegetable fermentation. The lactic acid bacteria go to work on the sugars and multiply throughout the milk. Soon after the milk has been taken over by these multiplying bacteria, the telltale tang of lactic acid begins to form. Enzymes begin to break down proteins and the product thickens a bit in the process.

Within just a couple of days you have clabber. Or, depending on how you chose to inoculate the milk, you can introduce a specific chain of bacteria in an attempt to coax the wild fermentation of clabber into a more controlled fermentation, giving you a familiar texture and flavor in yogurt, kefir or buttermilk.

Cheese is also a cultured dairy product and one that is often forgotten. While clabber, milk kefir and yogurt are the short-term solutions to preserving milk by culturing it, cheese is a longer-term solution. While cheesemaking in general is beyond the scope of this book, I am including one simple recipe for Simple Homestead Feta Cheese (page 132), simply because it is a means of preserving milk for several weeks through fermentation. Also, it's delicious.

SIMPLE, SUSTAINABLE HOME DAIRYING

When there are animals to be milked, crops to be planted, harvests to put up, water to haul and families to care for, complicated kitchen tasks are not an option. Milk has to be dealt with every single day to make the most of it, and it has to be turned into something edible beyond the tall, cold glass.

Simple solutions are therefore a must when you are getting started. This is sustainable home dairying—simple enough for the everyday; diverse enough to please all palates. The cultured dairy products that work within these confines are ones that produce more than one end product, self-perpetuate their own culture and require little hands-on time to make.

KEFIR: THE STAR OF MY HOMESTEAD KITCHEN

When there's too much milk in our kitchen, the first thing I make is kefir. When someone's got a bellyache or food poisoning, I turn to kefir. If you've got a skin rash or an unexplained ailment, I give you kefir. The simplicity, sustainability and health benefits of kefir are just too great to be ignored.

If you think you don't like the taste of kefir, then you may not have been given the right instructions on how to make it. There are several things you can do wrong in the process to produce a pungent kefir too strong for many palates. Conversely, there are a host of things you can do right to produce a smooth, tangy and subtle kefir. If that misconception is all that is holding you back, please try again with the instructions on page 125 for How to Make Milk Kefir. Kefir is simply too good for you and too simple to make to miss out on.

The reasons my affection for kefir run deep are many.

Easy to Make

Kefir is, by far, the easiest cultured dairy product to make—simpler than yogurt, butter or any cheese I've made. The grains used to make kefir are self-perpetuating, so they are a onetime purchase. It goes from start to finish in 24-hours max and the final product can be used to make a host of dairy products.

Multipurpose

Just because something is easy to make doesn't necessarily mean it is useful in the kitchen. Kefir, however, is. You can create four different dairy products from kefir and its grains:

1. Simply cultured kefir for drinking, smoothies, baking or dressing fruit and vegetable salads.

2. Thick, strained kefir for a Greek yogurt-like snack, a cream cheese-like spread or a sour cream-like dip.

3. Crème fraîche from cultured kefir (see page 138).

4. Soft and hard cheeses using kefir as the mesophilic culture (see page 132).

Beneficial Yeasts, Bacteria, B Vitamins and Kefiran

The versatility of kefir pales in comparison to the incredible benefits it brings to the human body. Of the many varieties of fermented foods we have consumed, we continually turn to kefir as an anchor for our daily well-being.

We have always found that drinking kefir gives us an almost-immediate energy. I put that down to the high B vitamin content and the enzymes that aid our digestion. That is why I like to serve it with heavier foods such as pancakes.

Milk kefir, when made from milk kefir grains, also contains a compound called *kefiran*. This compound is actually most abundant around the grains themselves, creating a noticeable viscous quality to the liquid surrounding the milk kefir grains. This polysaccharide has been found to be a powerful cancer-fighter (see http://www.ncbi.nlm.nih.gov/pubmed/26708130 for details).

Yeasts are much maligned, most likely due to the misunderstanding of concepts like candida overgrowth. Yeasts are all around us and inside us, so it is best to simply make friends with them and realize that their existence is part of a symbiosis in the natural world and within our bodies. The yeasts in milk kefir are considered to be the friendly types that work alongside the bacteria for optimal digestion.

And, of course, like all fermented foods, kefir has beneficial bacteria. Many find that the volume and range of bacteria in kefir are most beneficial to recolonizing the gut after a round of antibiotics or when dysbiosis is of concern. This may be due to the wide-ranging types of bacteria found in kefir and the fact that some of these strains may better survive the harsh, acidic reality of the stomach.

The Difference Between Yogurt and Kefir

But why not just eat yogurt? Yogurt is a probiotic-cultured food too. It is thick, creamy and fairly mild in flavor, depending on your starter. It takes a bit more effort to make than kefir, but not enough to deter the yogurt-lover in you. Like kefir, yogurt is certainly a wonderful cultured food, but the two are not the same.

Of the many fermented foods we have incorporated into our diets, nothing has worked as hard at fixing gut problems, giving energy and healing just about whatever ails us as kefir has. If our anecdotal support doesn't convince you, here are some scientific studies that may.

Kefir has more strains of bacteria, as described in a 2009 article (see http://depa.fquim.unam.mx/amyd/archivero/Kefir_1_12695.pdf). This is not uncommon when it comes to cultured foods that utilize a tangible culture starter (such as a kombucha SCOBY, water kefir grains or milk kefir grains). The wide-ranging types of bacteria perform a host of duties both in the kefir, as it ferments, and in the stomachs of those that imbibe it.

Kefir has kefiran, a polysaccharide found abutting the kefir grains. This substance has shown promise in treating both metabolic syndrome and leukemia (see http://www.ncbi.nlm.nih.gov/pubmed/27384318 for more information on metabolic syndrome and http://www.ncbi.nlm.nih.gov/pubmed/26708130 on leukemia).

Kefir contains beneficial yeasts that yogurt does not. Yogurt is primarily an anaerobic fermentation, meaning that the microorganisms present are mostly bacterial. Kefir, on the other hand, has a symbiosis of bacteria and yeasts—much like kombucha—that exist in harmony both in the kefir grains and the cultured milk kefir.

DAIRY-FREE MILK KEFIR

There are a very many people who do not have access to good milk or cannot tolerate it, so they wish to make kefir from dairy-free milk options. This is possible and can be a great way to reap the benefits of kefir for those with food intolerances.

For the benefit of your kefir grains, there is something to keep in mind, however. Milk kefir grains are designed to live off of the milk sugar lactose. When you put them into your milk, they begin to feast on the lactose and produce kefir, and they often multiply themselves through the process. They can go on indefinitely when fed properly with lactose-containing milk.

Unfortunately, dairy-free milk kefir can only be made with milk kefir grains in the short-term. Milk kefir grains may last a few months on coconut or nut milks but they will never multiply, and eventually the culture will die off due to a lack of lactose.

Another thing to consider is that dairy-free milks often contain very little or no sugar. You will therefore need to add 1 teaspoon (4 g) of a natural sugar source per quart of dairy-free milk when culturing non-dairy milk kefir.

Finally, be aware of the type of dairy-free milk you are culturing, the ingredients and the consequences of those ingredients to the culturing process. Almond milk is a very common dairy-free milk in grocery stores now but also contains many questionable ingredients. Homemade coconut and nut milks are much more reliable options for culturing.

With that in mind, you have a few options if you want to make dairy-free milk kefir:

1. Use your usual milk kefir grains to occasionally make dairy-free milk kefir. If much of the time you are feeding your grains dairy milk, they can, from time to time, be utilized to make dairy-free milks. To do this, simply take 1 to 2 tablespoons (7 to 15 g) of milk kefir grains and place them in one quart (1 L) of dairy-free milk to which you have added at least 1 teaspoon (4 g) of sugar. Allow to culture until tart, 12 to 18 hours. Non-dairy milk kefir may or may not thicken. Remove the grains and return them to the dairy milk to culture for at least a week before using them again in non-dairy milk. Note that this may strain your milk kefir grains, so you may want to use spare milk kefir grains for this while keeping another batch of grains exclusively for dairy milk.

2. Use spare milk kefir grains for a short-term culturing of non-dairy milks. Place 1 to 2 tablespoons (7 to 15 g) of kefir grains in 1 quart (1 L) of non-dairy milk to which 1 teaspoon (4 g) of natural sweetener has been added. Allow to culture until tart, 12 to 18 hours. Non-dairy milk kefir may or may not thicken. Strain the non-dairy kefir from the grains and place the grains in a fresh batch of non-dairy milk to which 1 teaspoon (4 g) natural sweetener has been added. Your kefir grains may work to culture the non-dairy milk for weeks or even months, but eventually the culture will die off due to the lack of lactose. By the time this happens, you may have grown enough milk kefir grains in dairy milk to start the process over again.

MILK: YOUR MOST IMPORTANT INGREDIENT

There is little you could do to repair a simple cheese or fermented dairy product when the milk itself is either of poor quality or is not the right milk for the job. It goes without saying, therefore, that your yogurt, kefir and cheese, along with the foods you make from these ingredients, are only as good as the milk you start with.

Obviously the ideal milk choice is the kind that comes straight from the animal. All of the recipes in this book were tested with raw milk straight from our animals or our neighbors' animals. I would encourage you to seek out similar milk for your family purely because it is the most unadulterated form of the food.

With that said, yogurt, kefir and simple cheeses can all be made with raw or pasteurized cow or goat's milk, with the former often being homogenized as well. There may be small nuances in flavor and texture when choosing between these types of milk, though it is only detectable to those familiar with all varieties. Specifically, non-homogenized cow's milk will have a cream layer in the final product, as it will separate during the culturing process. Furthermore, pasteurized milk always has more of a "cooked" milk flavor that is only slightly detectable to even the inexperienced palate.

On the question of full-fat or skimmed milk, full-fat is my choice as it is the most unadulterated. It is also actually linked to a lower incidence of diabetes (see http://circ.ahajournals.org/content/early/2016/03/22/CIRCULATIONAHA.115.018410.abstract for details). Goat milk is naturally homogenized and generally does not separate, so it cannot be skimmed, meaning that low-fat is just not an option for the simple home dairy raising goats. You could, of course, skim a good bit of the fat from the cow's milk to make butter, but leaving as much fat in the milk as you can will create a creamier, thicker fermented dairy and cheese.

What's Up with Ultra-Pasteurized Milk?

The many ways in which milk and cream are pasteurized is a complicated list put forth by the FDA. Regular pasteurization holds the milk's temperature at around 162°F (72°C) while ultra-pasteurization is a quick push to a whopping 280°F (138°C), followed by an almost instantaneous cooldown. The reasoning behind this brute force-type of pasteurization? Shelf life. The only benefit to this type of pasteurization is that you can have a container of milk available to consumers for up to 70 days, rather than pasteurized milk's average shelf life of two to three weeks. And it is not without its drawbacks. This unnatural surge of heat changes many of the textural and flavor components of milk, thereby encouraging producers to add thickeners and stabilizers to it. And if you desire to culture with it, be prepared for disappointing if not disastrous results. Neither cheeses nor cultured dairy products set up well when made with ultra-pasteurized milk. The reason for such poor results is most likely the damage done to the proteins when heated so aggressively and to such a high temperature.

STRAINING CULTURED DAIRY

For all of the cultured dairy products–kefir, yogurt, buttermilk, clabber–part of the liquid can be strained to create a thickened dairy product akin to Greek yogurt or cream cheese. The liquid that drips out is called *whey*, while the thickened dairy product is called *curds*.

While this process alone can greatly broaden the ways in which you can use cultured dairy products, it is really rather simple.

You need a deep bowl to catch the whey. This bowl should be narrow enough at the opening to hold a large plastic or stainless steel strainer. Place the strainer atop the bowl and line it with several layers of cheesecloth, a coffee filter or a clean tea towel.

Pour the yogurt, kefir, clabber or buttermilk into the lined strainer. If you wish to strain a large quantity, you may have to wait until some of the whey has dripped out of the curd before you can add more. Cover the top of the cultured dairy with either the corners of the cheesecloth or towel or with a separate coffee filter or lid.

Allow the cultured dairy to drip for a few hours for a Greek yogurt-like consistency or overnight for a thick cream cheese-like consistency. Keep in mind that the thicker your initial product, the thicker and more abundant the strained curds will be.

In the end you will have two products–the curds and the whey. Unless you have an immediate application for the whey, you will want to purify it for optimal storage time, especially if you do not have refrigeration. You simply need to make sure that all of the white dairy solids have been removed from the whey. If you see a bit of white or cloudiness in the whey, simply strain it again, this time through a coffee filter or tea towel. The final product should be a yellowish, completely translucent liquid.

Whey will keep for several months in the refrigerator or for up to a week if left at cool room temperature. The curds should be used right away or refrigerated for up to a week.

Six Ways to Use Whey

Whey is both very versatile and healthful. Containing plenty of hydrating factors, beneficial enzymes and bacteria and amino acids, whey has long been used alongside broth for the ill or infirm among us. So don't throw out that whey! Here are several uses for it.

Drink it. Whey can be sipped as is, though it is not for the faint of heart. You can stir a bit of honey or fruit juice into it for a supreme hydration drink.

Blend it. Throw whey and fruit into a blender for a simple smoothie.

Bake with it. Whey can be used in place of the liquid in bread recipes with good results.

"Cook" with it. Heating whey too much will kill much of the beneficial organisms. It can be used, however, in cold soups and salad dressings to lend a bit of tang.

Ferment other foods with it. Whey holds a great deal of the beneficial living organisms of the original cultured dairy. It can therefore be used to ferment other foods. Grains, vegetables and fruit can all use a bit of whey for fermentation, though keep in mind that the addition of whey to vegetable fermentation may alter both the flavor and bacterial profile (see On Starter Cultures on page 31).

Throw it in your compost bin to add some extra bacteria or feed it to your chickens or pigs.

EQUIPMENT

Cleanliness First

Although we are just skirting on the periphery of full-on home dairying in this book, much of the same need for cleanliness applies. Remember that we are dealing with bacteria here—the beneficial kind—and we are attempting to harness it to create delicious dairy products. What we don't want is to add competitive bacteria to the mix.

So cleanliness is of the utmost importance. Sterilization is a personal choice, in my opinion. Because I reject the germ theory and generally feel that sterilization is counterproductive to creating a symbiosis of beneficial bacteria between humans and environment, I generally don't sterilize my fermentation vessels and other equipment. But you certainly can.

With that said, clean equipment that has recently been washed with hot, soapy water is always a good idea. Just be sure to rinse the soap well and avoid antibacterial soaps.

Pots, Vessels and Utensils

In heating milk for yogurt or stirring curds for cheese, you will have to choose what type of utensils you will use. Stainless steel is acceptable, as long as the contact isn't prolonged. So heating, stirring and straining with stainless steel is not a problem.

Always use stainless steel pots in home dairying, but be careful to avoid aluminum. The acidic nature of cultured dairy will react with aluminum and leech this harmful heavy metal into your food.

Culturing is best done in glass jars of the pint (0.5-L), quart (1-L) and half-gallon (2-L) varieties. Earthenware or plastic can also be used, though the porous nature of these materials can make thorough cleaning difficult. Wooden spoons, plastic spatulas and stainless steel utensils are all acceptable for stirring and mixing cultured dairy.

Stainless steel and plastic strainers are recommended for straining kefir (remember that your kefir grains will come into daily contact with them!) and for making curds and whey. Various sizes are useful, though a small size, such as 2 to 3 inches (50 to 76 mm) in diameter is best used for making kefir.

Cheesecloth, butter muslin or clean tea towels are all useful for straining curds from whey, with the latter two being my personal choice. Coffee filters can also be used when you are straining small quantities.

A small cheese mold is useful for making feta cheese or for turning your strained clabber, kefir or yogurt into a harder cheese. There is no need for a cheese press for such applications.

If you intend to make cultured butter, you can use a small butter mold, though it is not necessary. Wooden butter paddles can also be used, though a wooden spoon or wooden spatula can also do the job just fine.

ABOUT THE RECIPES

Fermented dairy is only truly useful if it can be used to feed your family on a daily basis. This means it has to be dynamic in its application and delicious in its execution. Using cultured dairy for everything from breakfast to salad dressings to desserts is important to me as a homesteader, paying homage to the work that happens in the pasture and the milking stand.

But these applications must also be simple enough that my many other responsibilities allow for the making of these foods. And, of course, they must taste delicious so that in the end we can come together around the table and truly enjoy this food and appreciate where it comes from.

The tutorials will get you started in making Yogurt (page 127), Kefir (page 125), Cultured Butter (page 155), Buttermilk (page 156) and Clabber (page 154). The recipes that follow are how I create delicious, sustainable and diverse meals for our family using our favorite cultured dairy products. I make no secret of our family's love of milk kefir, but I encourage you to substitute whatever cultured dairy products you make regularly for the yogurt, kefir, buttermilk and sour cream in these recipes.

You will find three of our favorite breakfasts in this chapter: Kefir Pancake Syrup (page 138), Sprouted Buckwheat-Berry Cultured Dairy Smoothie (page 141) and Kefir Buckwheat Muesli (page 131). They are so alive with bubbles and bacteria that you'll wonder how you started your day any other way.

If you simply want to sip more kefir, I share how a second fermentation mellows it out while adding a punch of delicious flavor in Easy-Sipping Second Ferment Kefir (page 150).

You will find the hearty Lemony Spiced Chicken and Potato Salad (page 149) along with Fruit and Yogurt Slaw (page 136) and a favorite Yogurt Caesar Salad Dressing (page 146). All of these salads have cultured dairy as the main component, replacing most other oils or commercial sour cream. The German Sweet Potato Kefir Mash (page 152) is also a favorite main dish, with all of the flavors of a German potato salad but all of the goodness of homegrown sweet potatoes and kefir.

You will find the simple feta cheese I make for our family over and over again because it is both delicious and can be kept in a brine on the counter for weeks without any refrigeration. I also share with you how to use kefir to replace other purchased mesophilic cultures for cheesemaking. And then you will find a favorite rich and creamy dessert in Fruit and Yogurt Mousse (page 145).

All of this is to say that these recipes come from our family's table, where cultured dairy can sometimes be found at every meal of the day.

How to Make Milk Kefir

Milk kefir is a cultured dairy product believed to have originated in the Caucasus Mountains. Traditionally it is made with kefir grains, which will multiply and live as long as they are fed every 24 hours or so. Powdered milk kefir cultures also exist, although they are generally of the direct-set variety that can be used to reculture subsequent batches up to five to seven times before a new culture must be purchased.

The cycle of milk kefir is generally a 12- to 24-hour one, depending on how far you want the fermentation to go. At 12 hours, the milk kefir is mildly tangy and slightly thickened like cultured buttermilk. At 24 hours, it is stronger in flavor and sometimes thickens to the point of beginning to separate into curds and whey. With that in mind, you can choose your culturing period.

 Makes: 1 quart (946 ml) / Fermentation Time: 12 to 24 hours

1 quart (946 ml) room temperature milk

2-4 tsp (10-20 ml) milk kefir grains or direct-set culture

Combine the milk and milk kefir grains or direct-set culture in a quart-size (1-L) jar. Stir gently with a wooden spoon. Cover the jar with a clean cloth or coffee filter and fasten it down with a canning ring or rubber band. Place it out of the way to culture for 12 to 24 hours or until it has set up into a drinkable yogurt consistency.

If you have used a direct-set culture, you can simply use the kefir as is, reserving the amount noted on the package to reculture it. If you have used milk kefir grains, place a funnel into a clean quart (1-L) jar and put a stainless steel or plastic strainer on the funnel. Stir or shake the milk kefir until it is pourable and then pour it slowly through the strainer, stirring the kefir in the strainer with a wooden spoon or plastic spatula as you go, in order to move the kefir through the strainer.

You should now be left with milk kefir grains in the strainer and a quart of freshly cultured kefir. Put the milk kefir grains into fresh milk—no need to rinse them!—and repeat the culturing process. The quart of freshly cultured kefir can be refrigerated for up to 2 weeks, flavored and bottled for a second fermentation (see Easy-Sipping Second Ferment Kefir on page 150), or consumed within 2 to 3 days of culturing.

(continued)

Troubleshooting

Q. I really don't like the way my kefir tastes!

A. There are two tricks to making better-tasting kefir. The first is simply a matter of ratio. Although you can use a good amount of kefir grains to culture a quart (946 ml) of milk, it is not only unnecessary, but can also result in some strong kefir flavor.

In my time working as a consultant for Cultures for Health, the following tip has changed the game for kefir-makers over and over again. That tip is simple: Use fewer kefir grains to culture your quart (1 L) of milk. I find that a range of 2 teaspoons to 2 tablespoons (10 to 30 ml) is the most you would want to use in a quart of milk. As your kefir grains grow, stick with this ratio and use those grains in a separate quart of milk, giving some to a friend or feeding them to farm animals or the compost pile.

My other tip is that what people often find unpleasant about kefir is not its tang, but the yeast flavor it can have. It does take some getting used to, but it can also be avoided if you are really averse to it. For less yeasty flavors, give the milk kefir less access to oxygen. You can do this by replacing the permeable coffee filter or cloth you might use otherwise with a plastic lid left unscrewed. Less oxygen generally equals less yeast. Furthermore, a shorter fermentation time of twelve hours may be a better starting point as the kefir generally has a less potent flavor with a shorter fermentation period.

Q. The grains aren't multiplying or the kefir is taking longer to culture than expected.

A. Not all kefir grains multiply, especially those that have been dehydrated. But if yours are not multiplying, it could also be because the kefir isn't culturing evenly. Oftentimes the grains will sink to the bottom of the milk, so the couple of inches surrounding these grains culture quickly while the remaining milk just sits on top, separated from the grains. To avoid this, it is helpful to give milk kefir a swirl every now and again during the culturing process.

Q. The cultured milk kefir has thickened too much! How am I supposed to strain off the milk kefir grains?

A. This is actually fairly common, especially when you allow the kefir to ferment for a full 24 hours or in warmer temperatures. The best way to proceed is to put a waterproof lid on your jar and then shake the cultured kefir with the kefir grains still in it. This breaks up any curds that have formed and turns the kefir into a pourable consistency. Once it has been given a good shake, proceed with pouring the liquid kefir through the strainer to catch the milk kefir grains.

Occasionally when kefir is left to ferment for too long or the temperatures are warmer than expected, kefir will jump quickly to a separated curds-and-whey state. This is an indication that the kefir is overly acidic, probably having been left to culture too long, and the kefir grains need to be removed immediately and replenished in fresh milk. The tricky part is getting the grains out of the curds. Shaking the jar does not improve the situation when the curds are fully separated. Instead, I like to pour the whole lot into a bowl and fish out the milk kefir grains with clean hands. It's not pretty, but it is pretty much your only option. The upside is that the curds and whey can be strained to form a thick kefir cheese fairly easily at this point.

Q. There is a fuzzy white mold on the surface of my kefir.

A. Most likely, this is a harmless yeast. Harmful molds generally come in crazy colors and have strong odors. Give your milk kefir a sniff. Most likely it will have a strong yeast aroma but should not smell rotten. If this is the case, you can simply scrape the fuzz from the top of the kefir and strain the grains. If this is a reoccurring issue, you may have a bit of a yeast imbalance in your kitchen or in your kefir grains. I find that it helps to culture the kefir just long enough for it to thicken (12 to 16 hours) and attempt to lower the yeast balance by using a loosely fastened plastic lid rather than a permeable cloth or coffee filter during the fermentation.

Four Methods for Making Yogurt

The general process for making yogurt is simple and can be applied to any of the methods below that you choose to use. Because we like raw cultured dairy as well as thick, creamy yogurt, I make both raw milk kefir and homemade yogurt using the heating instructions below. While I find that this gives us the best of both worlds, see the instructions at the end of this recipe for how to make thick raw-milk yogurt if that is your goal.

Before you get started, the other thing to keep in mind is that there are two types of yogurt starter. The thermophilic starter is the most widely used and quite simply, it contains the type of bacteria that proliferate at warm temperatures (100 to 115°F [38 to 46°C]). If you are using store-bought yogurt as a starter, consider it thermophilic. The other type of starter is mesophilic. This type of starter can culture at room temperature. Instructions for using it can be found at the end of this tutorial.

Heat, Cool and Inoculate the Milk

Turning the heat up on the milk accomplishes two things:

1. It denatures the proteins. Simply put, it changes the structure of the milk, encouraging it to coagulate into the creamy curds we desire.

2. It eliminates any competing bacteria that might eventually weaken your starter. The bacterial balance of yogurt starter is delicate, and raw milk contains enough beneficial bacteria to nudge out the bacteria we are hoping to inoculate the milk with.

For the thickest yogurt, heat the milk to 180°F (82°C) and hold it there for as long as you can without letting the bottom scorch. You can place a cheese thermometer into your milk to test the temperature, or simply watch it. Milk reaches 180°F (82°C) just before it begins to boil so look for little bubbles around the edge. If you lose track of your heating and the milk begins to boil, do not fret. It will still make yogurt but may have a slightly different texture in the end.

Once the milk is heated, cool it down to 110 to 115°F (38 to 46°C) so that when the culture is added, it does not kill the bacteria. Again, you can use a thermometer or you can do a simple test with a clean finger. The milk is cool enough when you can hold a finger in it without feeling uncomfortably hot.

Once the milk is cool, add your culture starter. This can be 2 tablespoons (30 ml) of store-bought yogurt with live active cultures or a powdered culture starter you have purchased. In either case, just make sure that the starter is stirred into the milk very well so that it dissolves and the bacteria are evenly distributed.

Finally, choose your incubation method. The following methods can be used to make delicious, creamy, thick yogurt. Note that when gelatin is called for, it is in conjunction with making *raw* milk yogurt only.

Keeping Your Yogurt Raw

Obviously, if you want raw yogurt, you should skip the heating step. The thing about raw-milk yogurt is that it will never be thick like heated-milk yogurt. You can, however, add things like gelatin to thicken it up to a spoonable consistency. So if you wish to make raw-milk yogurt, simply heat the milk to the 110°F (38°C) mark to warm it without killing any enzymes.

To thicken raw-milk yogurt using gelatin, use 2½ teaspoons (11 g) of powdered gelatin for every quart (946 ml) of milk. To do this, set aside ½ cup (118 ml) of cold or room temperature milk and sprinkle the gelatin over it while you warm the remaining milk to 110°F (38°C). Once the milk has reached that temperature, whisk in the gelatin-milk mixture thoroughly. Proceed with the culturing process as you usually would, using any of the incubation methods listed.

Four Methods for Making Yogurt (continued)

Method: Electric Yogurt Maker

Commercial yogurt makers come in various sizes and with varying price ranges. If you want to make raw-milk yogurt, be sure that the manufacturer states that the temperature does not exceed 110 to 118°F (43 to 47 °C) at any point during the culturing period.

This is one of the easiest ways to make raw thermophilic yogurt. Simply heat the milk gently to 110°F (43°C), add ¼ cup (59 ml) of store-bought live yogurt or other thermophilic yogurt culture and gelatin, if using. Whisk vigorously and pour it into the yogurt maker's vessels. Allow to culture according to the manufacturer's instructions.

If you'd like to heat your milk, warm the milk to 180°F (82°C) and then cool to 110°F (43°C) before transferring it to yogurt maker. Omit gelatin.

Method: Homemade Makeshift Yogurt Incubator

If you do not own a commercial yogurt maker, the incubation conditions can be mimicked at home with some simple equipment.

One option is to use a cooler with a heat source. The cooler traps the heat, giving the thermophilic yogurt a warm environment to culture in. As the heat source, you can use either a heating pad set on low or hot water.

If using the heating pad, plug it in and set it on low and lay it in the bottom of the cooler. Warm and cool your milk, add the culture starter and gelatin, if using, and seal the jars. Place these on top of the heating pad and close the cooler as far as you can with the heating pad cord running from the cooler. Culture for 12 to 24 hours.

If using warm water, hot tap water is generally the right temperature. Simply place your 110°F (43°C) milk, culture starter and gelatin, if using, in sealed jars. Put these jars into the cooler and pour hot water around them, up to a couple of inches (50 mm) below the jar lids. After 12 hours, either remove the yogurt or replace the cooled water with a fresh batch of hot water and incubate for the remaining 12 hours.

This same process can be achieved in a large pot of warm water wrapped with a towel for insulation.

Method: Slow Cooker

Oh yes, you can make yogurt in your slow cooker! And, not surprisingly, it is one of the simplest, most hands-off methods out there. Note that this does not produce raw milk yogurt.

For a Two-Quart (2-L) Slow Cooker

Turn your slow cooker to low and pour in a half-gallon (1.9 L) of milk.

Heat on low for 2½ hours.

Once 2½ hours have elapsed, turn your slow cooker off and unplug it. Let the milk cool in the crock with the lid on for 3 hours.

After 3 hours, remove 1 to 2 cups (237 to 473 ml) of the warmed milk and place it in a bowl. Add ½ cup (118 ml) of yogurt with live active cultures and mix very well. Pour the yogurt-milk mixture back into the milk and whisk thoroughly.

Place the cover back on the slow cooker and wrap the entire slow cooker in a thick bath towel or two. Let it culture overnight, 8 to 12 hours.

In the morning, stir the yogurt (if desired) and store in glass quart (1-L) jars or a container of your choice.

For optimum texture, refrigerate for at least eight hours before using.

Method: Countertop

Mesophilic Countertop Yogurt

A simpler method you can use to make yogurt is to make it right on the countertop using a mesophilic culture specifically designed to culture at room temperature. These cultures can be reused as long as they are cared for properly. They can also be utilized in making raw-milk yogurt but the culture must be perpetuated with pasteurized milk to keep the organisms in the raw milk from competing with the yogurt culture.

To make countertop yogurt, heat the milk and then cool it to room temperature for a thicker texture. Otherwise fresh milk—at room temperature or chilled—can be mixed with a small portion of the culture, as indicated by the instructions accompanying your culture. Then cover the mixture and allow it to culture at room temperature (65 to 75°F [18 to 24°C]) for 8 to 24 hours.

The culture itself remains separate from the yogurt and can then be kept pure and used to make successive batches of yogurt. It will have to be multiplied from time to time using pasteurized milk. Note that grocery-store yogurt is generally made from thermophilic starters and as such cannot be used as a starter for this mesophilic yogurt.

Hot Climate Off-Grid Yogurt

If you live in a hot climate that hovers near triple-digit temperatures, the ambient temperature allows the yogurt to culture with no added equipment. Simply heat the milk, allow it to cool until it passes the finger test and inoculate it with a thermophilic starter. Once the milk and starter are well combined, seal the vessels and wrap the jars in a towel. Leave them on your countertop to culture for 8 to 24 hours or, if your home is air conditioned, put them outside, out of the sun and in a safe place.

Kefir Buckwheat Muesli with Figs and Ginger

You know you are starting the day off right when you pop the top off of your breakfast cereal and it is bubbling like mad. Those bubbles indicate life—probiotics, enzymes and easily assimilated nutrients. That is one reason that this is one of our favorite breakfast dishes. The other reason is that it is so, so yummy. Feel free to switch up the flavorings and dried fruits in this recipe.

 Makes: 6 to 8 servings / Fermentation Time: 24 hours (includes soaking time)

3 cups (51 g) buckwheat groats

3 cups (710 ml) cultured kefir (page 125)

Thumb-size piece ginger

12 dried figs

To serve: Fresh fruit, seeds, nuts, honey or sweetener of choice

Soak the buckwheat groats in 6 cups (1.4 L) of water for 12 to 24 hours. Drain but do not rinse; the starchy liquid will help with the fermentation.

In a half-gallon (2-L) vessel, combine the buckwheat groats, kefir, ginger and figs. Mix well to combine. Cover and allow to ferment for 12 to 24 hours. If it is a warmer time of the year, be sure to check it every 8 to 12 hours to see if the jar needs to be burped.

Once fermented, you can stash this cereal in the refrigerator for a day or two or serve it up. To serve, divide the muesli among 6 or 8 serving bowls. Top with fresh fruit, nuts, seeds and a drizzle of honey for a living, refreshing breakfast.

Simple Homestead Feta Cheese

A cheese that sits on the counter in a brine for several weeks, with no need for refrigeration or a fancy cheese cave is a cheese for me. Because of its simplicity and forgiving nature, this is the only cheese I make regularly (besides kefir and yogurt cheese). If you like flavorful cheese and don't want to fuss with complicated recipes, this one's for you too.

 Makes: Approximately ½ pound (227 g) / Fermentation Time: 48 hours / Storage Time: 2 to 4 weeks at room temperature

½ gallon (1.9 L) fresh milk

¼ tsp mesophilic culture or 1 tbsp (15 ml) kefir (page 125)

½ tsp rennet mixed into ¼ cup (59 ml) water

⅓ cup (80 g) salt and 2 cups (474 ml) water or whey, for brine

Heat the milk to approximately 85°F (29°C), or barely warm to the touch. If you are working with milk fresh from the pail, you can omit the heating step. Add the culture and whisk carefully to completely combine. Cover with a lid and leave to culture for 1 hour.

Mix the rennet and water together and pour into the cultured milk. Stir for 1 to 2 minutes. Cover the pot again and let sit overnight, or for 8 to 12 hours.

In the morning, the curds and whey should be slightly separated and you should be able to break it cleanly when inserting a knife or finger into the curd.

Line a colander with several layers of cheesecloth, butter muslin or a clean tea towel. Place the colander into a larger bowl set in a sink in order to save the whey.

Cut the curd into ½-inch (13-mm) cubes in both directions and stir for 1 to 2 minutes. Pour the curds into the lined colander and allow the whey to drip through.

Gather up the cheesecloth and hang the cheese over a bowl for 12 hours at room temperature (65 to 85°F [18 to 29°C]). Save 2 cups (473 ml) of the whey for the brine. After 12 hours, flip the cheese over and allow it to hang an additional 12 hours.

Salt the cheese on all sides and place in a sealable container. Seal and let sit at room temperature for an additional 24 to 48 hours or until firm and ready for brine.

Make a strong brine using the salt and water or whey saved from straining the curds. Once the cheese is drained, cut into ½ to 1-inch (13- to 25-mm) pieces and place in the brine. It's okay if the cheese crumbles a bit. The cheese can now be stored for 2 to 4 weeks at room temperature or 1 to 2 months in the refrigerator, as long as it stays under the brine.

Okroshka

I know this sounds like the oddest thing you have ever heard of, but it really works and works well. And this is coming from a family who does not particularly like cold soups. I like to throw this together with leftovers as a super-simple meal. Feel free to vary the meat, potato and vegetable components to whatever is seasonal or you have on hand.

 Makes: 4 servings

2 medium russet potatoes, diced into ¼-inch (6-mm) cubes

6 slices bacon

1 medium cucumber, peeled, seeded and diced

6 radishes, halved and thinly sliced

4 scallions, sliced (white and green parts)

1 tsp (5 g) sea salt, more to taste

1½ cups (355 ml) kefir (page 125)

1½ cups (355 ml) water

2 heaping tbsp (5 g) minced fresh dill

1 garlic clove, minced

Juice of ½ lemon

Place diced potatoes into a small saucepan. Cover them with water and bring to a boil over high heat. Cover the pan, turn the heat down to medium, and simmer for approximately 5 minutes, or until potatoes are tender but not mushy. Diced leftover boiled or baked potatoes also work well.

Meanwhile, place bacon in a small cast-iron skillet over low heat and fry until crisp, flipping once. Remove to a plate and allow to cool.

While the potatoes and bacon are cooking, prepare the cucumber, radishes and scallions and add them to a large soup pot or serving bowl. Mix together the salt, kefir, water, dill and garlic and pour the mixture over the vegetables.

Once the potatoes are no longer hot (they don't burn your fingers when you touch them), add them to the rest of the ingredients and crumble in the bacon.

Add the lemon juice and stir gently to combine. Taste and add seasoning as needed.

Serve with sourdough bread and butter for a light but satisfying meal.

Fruit and Yogurt Slaw

Sweet, tart and packed with flavor, this is the creamy coleslaw we grew up eating but with a way better ingredient list. No mayonnaise or added oils are necessary when you use whole milk yogurt and fresh produce. Serve as a side dish at a family barbecue or throw on some grilled meat for a main dish salad.

 Makes: 6 to 8 servings

8 cups (2.7 kg) shredded cabbage, packed

1 tsp (5 g) salt

½ large red onion, minced

1½ cups (225 g) chopped sweet-tart apple such as Honeycrisp or McIntosh

⅓ cup (13 g) roughly chopped parsley, packed

DRESSING

¾ cup (177 ml) whole milk yogurt (page 125)

1 tsp (5 ml) Dijon mustard

2 tsp (10 ml) raw honey

1 tbsp (15 ml) apple cider vinegar, or more if your yogurt is not particularly tart

½ tsp sea salt, or to taste

½ tsp ground black pepper

Combine the cabbage and salt in a large bowl. Cover and allow to sit for at least 1 hour to allow some of the liquid to be drawn out. Squeeze the liquid from the cabbage and discard. Give the cabbage a quick rinse to remove the excess salt.

Combine cabbage, onion, apple and parsley together in mixing bowl. Combine the ingredients for the dressing in a separate bowl and stir. Pour three-fourths of the dressing over the cabbage mixture and toss together. Taste and add the remaining dressing
as needed.

Serve straight away or refrigerate for up to 1 day before serving.

Kefir Pancake Syrup

Sensible, sustainable eating habits are my mainstay so I neither seek out nor attempt to create recipes that are the "ultimate" version of that particular food. But this pancake syrup, my friends, has given me by far the best pancake experience of my life. Warm sourdough pancakes topped with generous pats of grass-fed butter and this tangy-sweet syrup are the umami of pancakes. Seriously. Oh, and it turns pancakes into breakfast fuel instead of breakfast bricks.

Makes: 2⅓ cups (554 ml)

2 cups (474 ml) cultured kefir (page 125), at room temperature

⅓ cup (80 ml) maple syrup, at room temperature

½ tsp vanilla extract

Combine all ingredients in a small pitcher and pour generously over buttered Sourdough Pancakes (page 99). Enjoy a brand-new take on pancakes.

VARIATION: I often substitute gently warmed raw honey for the maple syrup.

Kefir Crème Fraîche

Because kefir is a mesophilic culture and therefore can be used to culture both cream and cheese (see Kefir as a Mesophilic Cheese Culture on page 153), I had to make this simple version of sour cream. It is just one more reason kefir is the king of cultured dairy in my kitchen.

 Makes: One pint (473 ml) / Fermentation Time: 12 to 24 hours /
Storage Time: 2 weeks refrigerated, 2 days otherwise

2 cups (474 ml) cream (not ultra-pasteurized)

¼ cup (59 ml) cultured kefir (page 125)

Combine cream and cultured kefir in a pint (0.5-L) jar. Stir gently but thoroughly with a nonreactive utensil. Cover the jar with a coffee filter, cloth or napkin, and fasten it tightly with a rubber band or canning ring.

Allow cream to culture at room temperature for 12 to 24 hour or until thick. During this period, it may separate a little. If this happens, simply stir it back together. It is fully cultured when it is as thick as whipped cream with a pleasantly tangy kefir flavor and aroma.

Store in the refrigerator for up to a couple of weeks or eat within a couple of days.

How to Ferment Grains with Kefir

Due to its bacterial and yeast content, milk kefir is a great medium for fermenting grains when you don't have a sourdough starter around. You can do this with whole grains such as brown or white rice, millet, oats, buckwheat, wheat, rye, barley and so forth. This can also be utilized for baked goods—wheat or gluten-free—in which baking powder or baking soda is used as additional leavening.

Whole Grains

Using a grain mill on a loose setting or a powerful blender, crack the whole grains so at least a bit of the starchy insides are opened up.

Mix the grains with twice their volume of water plus 2 tablespoons (30 ml) of milk kefir.

Cover loosely with a permeable lid and allow to ferment in a warm place for 1 to 3 days, depending on the temperature. The grains have fermented once they have a pleasantly sour aroma and they begin to show signs of bubbling.

To cook: Add fermented grains to the pot plus 1 cup (237 ml) of water for every cup (160 g) of dry, cracked grain you started with. Bring to a boil and reduce heat to a simmer. These will cook much more quickly than grains that have not been soaked or fermented. These should cook in approximately half the time as the same grain left unsoaked.

Flours and Baked Goods

For quick-bread recipes that utilize baking soda or baking powder as leavening, replace the liquid in the recipe (whether water or milk) with an equal quantity of milk kefir.

Mix the flour and milk kefir in a mixing bowl. Cover and leave to ferment for 12 to 24 hours. Add all remaining ingredients in the recipe you are using except the leavening agents. Stir until nearly combined and then sprinkle over baking soda or baking powder. Stir to combine.

To bake: Because the grains have fully hydrated, it may take an additional 5 to 10 minutes for the baked good to cook through, or 1 to 2 minutes for the pancakes to cook through. Lower the temperature by approximately 15 percent and expect it to take just a bit longer to cook through.

Sprouted Buckwheat-Berry Cultured Dairy Smoothie

Say that ten times fast. We love smoothies for their ability to sneak all sorts of goodness into a delicious drink—raw egg yolks, coconut oil and barley grass, for instance. The problem is that I usually have to serve them with some sort of baked good (or popcorn!) to fill my family up. Not with this smoothie! I throw soaked or sprouted buckwheat into the mix for a filling, delicious snack or breakfast. And feel free to sneak your favorite nutritional boosters in there as well.

 Makes: 4 to 6 servings / Fermentation Time: 56 hours (includes sprouting time)

1 cup (170 g) buckwheat groats, sprouted

1 quart (946 ml) whole milk yogurt, kefir, clabber or buttermilk

1 lb (450 g) fresh berries of your choice

1 banana

2 tbsp (30 ml) raw honey

1 tsp (5 ml) vanilla extract

Soak the buckwheat groats in 2 cups (474 ml) of water overnight. If you are pressed for time, you can stop there and use soaked buckwheat. If not, get a little more nutrition out of them by sprouting. To sprout, drain and rinse the groats and place in a sieve or sprouter, covered loosely to keep out bugs. Rinse buckwheat every 8 to 12 hours for 2 days or until tiny tails begin to emerge from the buckwheat groats.

Add all ingredients to the blender. Blend on high until smooth. Serve cold.

VARIATION: Steel-cut or rolled oats can be substituted for the buckwheat groats. These grains won't sprout like buckwheat but can be soaked in kefir or water and sourdough starter as per the instructions on page 139: How to Ferment Grains with Kefir.

Seasonal Vegetable Raita

When July beats down its relentless summer heat, there are very few foods that will bring anyone to the table. This is one of them. Tucking in seasonal vegetables from the garden is the best way to go, so feel free to use sweet peppers, tomatoes, broccoli, peas, beans or even the ubiquitous zucchini. And on the hottest of days, feel free to make a supper of this, a cold glass of raw milk and a vine-ripened watermelon.

Makes: 4 to 6 servings

1¾ cups (262 g) cucumber

¼ cup (38 g) radish

1 cup (237 ml) strained yogurt (page 121)

½ tsp each roughly ground cumin and coriander

2 green onions, minced

1 garlic clove, minced

Salt to taste

Combine the cucumber and radish in a colander set over a bowl. Sprinkle the vegetables liberally with salt and cover the colander with a dish towel. Leave to drain for at least 1 hour to release some of the moisture.

After the vegetables have drained, transfer them to a medium serving bowl. Add all of the remaining ingredients except the salt. Taste the raita and add salt only if needed. Serve alongside Sourdough Flatbreads (page 95), grilled meat of choice and Veg Brine Homestead Fermented Herb Sauce (page 217).

Fruit and Yogurt Mousse

Finding new and interesting ways to serve cultured dairy is important if it is a mainstay of your diet. This dessert does just that with seasonal fruit and freshly made yogurt. Much like a panna cotta, this creamy dessert is set with gelatin. Serve it in a big bowl family-style or pour into individual jars or ramekins for a special treat. Beware that a few fruits—namely kiwi, fig and pineapple—contain a protein-splitting enzyme that can keep the gelatin from setting. Berries, apples and stone fruits are all good choices.

Makes: 6 to 8 servings

Butter as needed for greasing bowl or serving bowls

1 quart (946 ml) homemade whole-milk yogurt (page 128), strained for 2–3 hours to thicken

¼ cup (60 ml) raw honey

2 tsp (10 ml) vanilla extract

2½ tsp (11 g) gelatin

6 tbsp (89 ml) milk

4 tbsp (59 ml) water, just off the boil

2 cups (300 g) chopped fresh, seasonal fruit

Lightly butter a 1½- to 2-cup (360- to 480-ml) glass serving bowl or enough jam jars or ramekins to contain 6 to 8 cups (1.4 to 1.9 L) liquid.

Whisk together the yogurt, honey and vanilla. Continue whisking for several minutes or until a bit fluffy from the introduction of air. Set aside.

Bloom the gelatin by filling a small bowl or measuring cup with the milk. Sprinkle the gelatin over and do not stir. Set aside for 5 minutes while you heat the water.

Whisk the gelatin into the milk. Quickly pour in the hot water while stirring. Quickly pour the gelatin mixture into the yogurt mixture and whisk well to combine. Fold the fruit in swiftly and pour into a greased bowl, jars or ramekins.

Yogurt Caesar Salad Dressing

In the unfortunate days when I always ordered salads from way too many restaurants, Caesar salad was my go-to choice. This dressing embodies a lot about the changes in my lifestyle from then to now. It contains no vegetable oils or eggs, though raw egg yolks are now right up my alley. Instead, thick yogurt and olive oil bring together the lemon, Parmesan and anchovy into a dressing I am very fond of.

Makes: Approximately 2 cups (473 ml)

2 flat anchovy fillets

2 medium garlic cloves, minced finely

¼–½ tsp salt, or to taste

½ cup (90 g) lightly packed, finely grated Parmesan cheese

¾ cup (184 g) whole-milk yogurt (page 128)

5 tbsp (74 ml) extra virgin olive oil

3–4 tbsp (44–59 ml) lemon juice, depending on the tartness of your yogurt

¼ tsp black pepper

In a small mixing bowl, mash the anchovy fillets, garlic and salt together with a fork until a paste forms. Mix in all other ingredients and whisk well. Taste and adjust the seasoning as needed.

Transfer to a pint (0.5-L) jar and serve with a crisp green salad or as a dip for veggies.

Lemony Spiced Chicken and Potato Salad

Salads like this are forever coming to my rescue in the kitchen. The potatoes, onions and chicken all cook together in a pot. The dressing gets mixed up and the greens chopped, and not long after that, it all gets tossed together into a delicious salad that is big on flavor. If ever there are garden potatoes and greens, rooster meat left over from making broth and homemade goat kefir, this dish is on the menu.

Makes: 6 to 8 servings

2 lb (907 g) potatoes, cubed

1 yellow onion, diced

2 boneless, skinless chicken breasts or 2 cups (459 g) cooked and cubed chicken

2 large bunches fresh organic spinach, stems removed

2 large garlic cloves, minced

Juice of 2 small lemons

1½ tsp (4 g) turmeric

½ tsp ground coriander

¼ tsp ground cayenne

¼ cup (60 ml) extra virgin olive oil

1½ cups (355 ml) kefir (page 125) or yogurt, strained (page 128) for 2 hours until slightly thickened

Salt to taste

Combine the potatoes and onion in a medium pot and mostly cover with water. Place the chicken breasts atop the potato-onion mixture, if using raw chicken, and place the lid on the pot. Put the pot over medium heat and cook until the potatoes are tender and the chicken is just cooked through and has reached a temperature of 165°F (74°C), approximately 15 minutes. Remove the chicken to a platter to cool, and drain the potatoes and onions and set aside.

Meanwhile, prepare the spinach by washing it and removing the stems. Add the spinach, garlic, lemon juice, turmeric, coriander and cayenne to a large salad bowl. Mix to combine.

Once the chicken is cool enough to handle, cut into bite-size cubes. Add the cooled but still warm potatoes, onions and chicken to the spinach mixture in the salad bowl.

Drizzle over olive oil and add kefir. Sprinkle everything with sea salt and stir gently to combine. Taste and adjust seasoning as needed.

VARIATION: Swiss chard is a great substitute for spinach. It is often my first choice as it grows so much more readily in our climate.

Easy-Sipping Second Ferment Kefir

A second fermentation is commonly used for fermented beverages like kombucha and water kefir for its ability to flavor and carbonate these delicious drinks. In the case of milk kefir, a second ferment not only flavors the kefir with whatever you wish, it also has a mellowing effect.

By removing the kefir grains, you protect them from any damage the flavorings might do while replenishing the grains in fresh milk. Covering the milk kefir during the second fermentation keeps oxygen out, which seems to mellow the yeast component of kefir.

I give one simple option we like, but the flavorings are only limited by your imagination. Use seasonal fruit, spices, flavored tea such as chai, extracts, herbs and herbal oils in your second ferment.

 Makes: 1½ cups (355 ml) / Fermentation Time: 12 to 24 hours

1½ cups (355 ml) cultured kefir (page 125)

½ tsp vanilla extract

Peel of 1 small organic orange

Add the kefir and vanilla extract to a pint (0.5-L) jar. Break up the orange peel into several pieces to release some of the oils and add them to the kefir mixture. Stir gently to combine and cover with a plastic lid that is left just a little bit loose.

Leave on the counter to culture for 12 to 24 hours. Remove the orange peels and serve immediately, with a sweetener if desired, or refrigerate for up to a week before serving.

VARIATIONS: Chai-Spiced Kefir: Use three chai tea bags in place of the orange peel.

Pumpkin Pie Kefir: Add ½ teaspoon of pumpkin pie spice in place of the orange peel.

Eggnog: Sprinkle in ¼ teaspoon of nutmeg in place of the orange peel and double the vanilla.

Berries and Cream: Add ⅓ cup (80 g) of berries in place of the orange peel.

German Sweet Potato-Kefir Mash

German potato salad is a dish from my youth, growing up in rural Minnesota. There is much about my homeland that I have taken with me to the Lone Star state, namely family and food. With Texas sweet potatoes and homemade kefir from our goats, this recipe bridges the gap between then and now in a most delicious way.

Makes: 4 to 6 servings

4 large sweet potatoes

4 strips bacon

8 green onions

¾ cup (177 ml) cultured kefir (page 125)

2 tbsp (30 ml) bacon drippings

1 tbsp (15 ml) apple cider vinegar

Salt to taste

Peel the sweet potatoes and cook, covered in water, until tender. Meanwhile, fry the bacon over medium-low heat until crispy. Once the potatoes and bacon are cooked, drain the potatoes and allow them to cool slightly. Set the bacon aside to cool as well.

Slice the green onions thinly and add to the warm (but not hot) sweet potatoes. Mix together the kefir, bacon, bacon fat and apple cider vinegar in a separate bowl and pour over the potato mixture. Mix together into a rough mash and season with salt to taste. Serve as a side dish with meat or along with a big salad for a delicious lunch.

Kefir as a Mesophilic Cheese Culture

I was making kefir and yogurt long before I delved into the practice of cheesemaking. After making several successful rounds of simple goat cheese, I started to wonder what exactly was in the cheese cultures I was using. These cheese cultures were touted as being mesophilic, after all, which made me wonder if other mesophilic cultures–like our beloved kefir– might be used interchangeably.

The answer was a resounding yes.

Cheese is generally made by adding a culture to milk, followed by rennet. The rennet is an enzyme that helps the milk to form a curd. It was traditionally taken from the stomach of a calf. Similarly, cheese was once made without the use of cheese cultures that come in shiny little packets. Instead, people used whatever bacteria was present in the milk, in a cultured dairy product they had also prepared, in the cheese cave and in the air surrounding the cheese operation.

Using kefir, therefore, as a starter for your cheesemaking is a simple solution that allows you to purchase one less ingredient. And the process is really simple.

To replace mesophilic cheese cultures with milk kefir, use 2 tablespoons (30 ml) cultured kefir for every half-gallon (1.9 L) of milk called for in a cheese recipe. Follow all other instructions, using kefir in place of a powdered culture starter.

Milk Clabber

Also known as bonny clabber or sour milk, this wild fermented milk is possibly the simplest way to transform milk into an edible food in a different form. Instead of inoculating milk with a specific strain of bacteria as you would yogurt or kefir, the milk is left to ferment naturally. While this recipe contains only one ingredient, it is imperative that it be raw milk, not pasteurized, as pasteurized milk does not contain any of the bacteria needed for the souring to occur properly.

Fermentation Time: 2 to 4 days

Raw milk

Place a quart (946 ml) or half-gallon (1.9 L) of raw milk on the counter and allow it to culture at room temperature for 24 to 48 hours, depending on the temperature. It is done when it has thickened up to the consistency of buttermilk or yogurt.

Clabber can then be used in place of buttermilk and other cultured dairy in baking and cooking. It can also be strained to make a cream cheese-like spread. Traditionally it was served with porridge or as a stand-alone breakfast with fruit or sugar. Clabber is best used within a day or two of souring, unless refrigeration is employed.

Curds and Whey

If you've ever heard of Little Miss Muffet, then you have probably heard of curds and whey. This is simply clabbered milk left to sour a bit longer or at warmer room temperature than its predecessor, clabber. The end result is slightly more acidic than clabber, which helps the curds separate from the whey.

Fermentation Time: 2 to 4 days

Raw milk

Leave milk to sour on the counter for 2 to 3 days in a warm space such as next to a wood or cook stove. The curds and whey are ready to use once the yellow whey has separated out from the thick curds.

This can be eaten as is with sugar, fruit or spice. The extensive separation of the curds from the whey makes it easy to strain off the whey for a soft cheese.

The whey itself is a valuable food product. It can be used to ferment other foods such as grains. It can be used as a culture starter for Whey Sodas (see page 172) or fermented vegetables, if so desired. It can also be used in smoothies or sweetened with honey as a refreshing probiotic beverage for hot days in the field.

To avoid more rapid spoiling, be sure to strain all of the milk solids from the whey. To do this, simply pour the whey through a coffee filter or sieve lined with a clean tea towel. Curds should be used within a day or two or refrigerated. Whey keeps for a couple of weeks at room temperature.

Cultured Butter and Traditional Buttermilk

It takes 2 to 4 gallons (7.6-15.1 L) of cow's milk to harvest the cream needed to make a pound (0.45 kg) of butter. Of course this is all dependent on the type of cow and the butterfat content of the milk, but this is a good average and something to consider when we purchase butter. Cultured butter is made from cultured or soured cream. You can skim the cream off the soured milk (clabber) or start with fresh cream, and then choose your method of making sour cream. Then make delicious butter, full of enzymes and beneficial bacteria, with this recipe. There are few things as delicious as rich, yellow, cultured butter with just a hint of tang.

Makes: 1 lb (450 g) butter plus buttermilk / Storage Time: 3 to 6 days at room temperature, several weeks in the refrigerator or several months in the freezer

4-5 cups (946-1,183 ml) cream

¼-½ tsp sea salt

Sour the cream. You can simply skim the cream from the clabber (see page 154), use sour cream (page 159) or start with sweet cream and then culture it with milk kefir grains, buttermilk or a previous batch of sour cream.

Churn the butter. You can do this by hand using a wooden churn, a glass jar churn fitted with a manual paddle attachment, or a quart (1-L) jar with a few marbles in it that you shake for an extended period of time. An electric stand mixer or food processor can also be used.

Churning is simply the process of beating or moving the cream around until the butterfat separates from the buttermilk. Fill the vessel of your choosing halfway to leave room for the whipped cream stage and start to churn. During this process, you will see the cream go through four stages: Soft peaked whipped cream; stiff peaked whipped cream; whipped cream with a coarse texture; butterfat separated from the buttermilk.

There is a distinctive sloshing sound made when the fourth stage is reached. If you are using an electric mixer with an open bowl, be prepared to be nearby when the butterfat separates. As soon as this stage starts, you will want to turn off the mixer to avoid spraying nearby countertops and cabinets with buttermilk.

Pour the buttermilk from the vessel into a quart (1-L) jar. This can then be used for fresh drinking or baking or for souring other foods. It will have a sour aroma and flavor.

Transfer the butter to a bowl, if needed, and wash the butter with cool water. To do so, submerge the butter in water and press it against the side of the bowl with a wooden spoon or clean hands as you work the buttermilk from it. Discard the cloudy water/buttermilk and repeat with fresh water. Continue to discard and replenish the water/buttermilk until it runs clear. Continue to work the butter to remove any remaining water.

Once the butter is washed and drained, mix in the salt. If this is your first time making butter, start with ¼ teaspoon of salt and adjust the amount to your taste as needed for future batches. Transfer the butter to a butter mold or form logs and wrap it in waxed paper. Use within several days or store in cold storage or a freezer for the time indicated above.

Cultured Buttermilk

What we now think of as cultured buttermilk is simply milk that has been inoculated with specific strains of bacteria and cultured at room temperature, much like kefir. Traditionally, buttermilk was actually the by-product of butter making and oftentimes, butter was made from soured or cultured cream. Thus buttermilk was a cultured food but not one made directly from the milk. With that in mind, let me present you with several options.

This is the type of buttermilk available in grocery stores. It is a mesophilic culture, meaning that it cultures at room temperature. Note that the same culture can be used to make sour cream. There are two options when it comes to a starter culture for cultured buttermilk.

 Makes: 1 quart (946 ml) / Fermentation Time: 12 to 24 hours

Direct-set culture starter

Store-bought buttermilk

1 quart (946 ml) milk (not ultra-pasteurized)

4 tbsp (20 ml) cultured buttermilk or direct-set culture (see below)

Combine the milk and culture starter of choice and mix thoroughly. Cover with a clean cloth or coffee filter and secure with a rubber band or canning ring. Place at warm room temperature (75 to 85°F [24 to 29°C]) for 12 to 24 hours. The buttermilk is cultured once it has thickened up.

Transfer to cold storage, where it will keep for a week before you need to reculture a new batch to perpetuate the starter. Will keep at room temperature for 2 to 3 days before beginning to separate.

DIRECT-SET CULTURE STARTER. This is generally a dried white powder that contains the bacteria necessary to culture the milk. These are nice because they are self-perpetuating, meaning that you culture it once and take a small amount from that batch, which can then inoculate the next batch. This is great if you want to make buttermilk frequently, as you will have to feed the culture at least weekly in order to keep it alive.

STORE-BOUGHT BUTTERMILK. If you only want buttermilk on occasion, purchasing a store-bought cultured buttermilk can work as your culture starter, much as store-bought yogurt can inoculate homemade yogurt. This can be used to culture several batches by saving a couple of tablespoons from each batch. In my experience, however, the culture begins to weaken after just a few rounds.

Sour Cream Three Ways

Soured milk and cream are a fact of life if you have dairy animals. There are myriad uses for this product, including applications outside the kitchen such as chicken, cat, dog and pig food. Sour cream, however, should never be fed to these animals unless you are flush in cream; it's just too good not to use for human consumption.

 Makes: 1 pint (473 ml) / Fermentation Time: 18 to 24 hours

FRESH, RAW CREAM

Cream (raw or pasteurized, not ultra-pasteurized)

CRÈME FRAÎCHE

2 cups (474 ml) cream (raw or pasteurized, not ultra-pasteurized)

2 tbsp (30 ml) cultured buttermilk (see page 156)

FRESH, RAW CREAM

For a wild fermentation, simply allow your milk to clabber and skim the cream from the top. Alternatively, start with sweet cream and allow it to sour for 24 to 48 hours as you would clabber. Note that this fermentation is unpredictable, as you are not inoculating it with any specific strains of bacteria. As such, the flavor may vary from batch to batch. One way to keep it a bit more consistent is to add a couple of spoons of a well-loved batch of naturally soured cream to the sweet cream as a culture starter for the next batch. In essence, you will have created your own preferred sour cream starter.

CREAM (RAW OR PASTEURIZED, NOT ULTRA-PASTEURIZED)

A mesophilic starter culture can be purchased and mixed into cream and cultured at room temperature. This will most likely have a similar flavor to commercial sour cream and is therefore a helpful way to introduce picky eaters to homemade sour cream. Culturing instructions and times given by the manufacturer should be followed.

CRÈME FRAÎCHE

This French cultured cream is usually richer and milder in tang than sour cream. If you are purchasing cream for this recipe, look for the cream with the highest fat content. This simple countertop culture is one of the easiest and tastiest ways to begin incorporating homemade probiotic foods into your family's meals.

Combine the cream and cultured buttermilk in a pint (0.5-L)- or quart (1-L)-size jar. Mix well to incorporate the two ingredients thoroughly. Cover the jar loosely with a plastic lid or fasten a clean cloth or coffee filter with a rubber band or canning ring.

Allow to culture for 18 to 24 hours or until thickened. Transfer to cold storage where it will keep for 1 to 2 weeks or eat it up within 3 days of culturing.

Beverages

It is not always easy to convey the reality of homestead life off-grid. Throughout these pages, I touch on ingredients harvested from the garden and preserved during times of plenty. I fear I may even edge toward perpetuating the romanticizing of a life such as this.

The reality is that some days are only filled with dirt and mud and crops that failed. Some weeks might see only perpetual dirty laundry, hauling water and tending to animals in unpleasant conditions. The first four years of life off-grid were, for us, seemingly fruitless . . . if success is measured in harvest baskets.

Thankfully we do not measure our success in terms of crop yields. The truth is that the seemingly hard times and hard work have broken us in the best possible way. They have solidified our reasons for doing this and shown us our need to walk this agrarian path.

During the early years, when little was harvested and eggs, rice and beans were staples, I continuously turned to cultured beverages like Water Kefir (page 181) and Kombucha (page 187) for nourishment. Kvasses (page 163) too have given us enzymes and probiotics when fresh salads and homegrown fermented vegetables were not an option.

Some years are plentiful and some are not, but we must take either circumstance with gratitude. A fizzy, fermented beverage doesn't hurt either.

HOW BEVERAGES FIT INTO A SUSTAINABLE FOOD SYSTEM

If you've ever known the reality of seasonal eating where monotony can often come as a plague when root vegetables and cabbage are your mainstay, a bottle of kvass or kombucha can completely change the outlook of your meal—and your digestion.

A big part of eating what you grow—or what is available locally—is using everything to its fullest potential in terms of both flavor and nutrition. Furthermore, fermented beverages are one of the easiest foods to convince naysayers to try. They are refreshing, slightly sweet (if you want them to be) and familiar to the Western palate.

Finally, they can easily become the only living food on the table in times of scarcity. The natural rhythm of the seasons demands that there be a time of plenty and a time of hunger. You may not be truly hungry, but you may end up eating primarily root crops and animal foods for a portion of the year, so that glass of kvass may be the only enzymatic and exciting element in a meal. These beverages, therefore, get you through the often less-than-glamorous reality of seasonal eating.

Besides that, they are dead simple to make.

THE STAGES OF BEVERAGE FERMENTATION

If you start with sugar, water and the tiniest bit of bacteria, you can soon have a fermented beverage on hand. Whether it is a "soft" lacto-fermented beverage, a hard alcoholic one or good old vinegar depends on sugar, time and exposure to oxygen. They all begin with sweet liquids, so let's discuss where we go from here.

Generally speaking, sugar- or fruit-based beverages go through several stages of fermentation.

Fresh juice -> soft drink (primarily lactic acid fermentation) -> hard drink (more alcohol content) -> vinegar

Take apple cider, for instance. It begins as freshly pressed apple juice, more or less. If left for a short amount of time, it changes to soft cider when the lactic acid bacteria have taken over. The beverage contains only trace amounts of alcohol along with beneficial bacteria, enzymes and small amounts of organic acids. This is primarily a lactic acid fermentation.

Given a bit more time, this soft drink will begin to form more alcohol. Eventually it contains enough alcohol to no longer be considered a soft drink. At this point, the sweetness is minimal and the alcohol flavor is pronounced. This is now primarily an alcohol fermentation known as hard cider.

The final stage can only happen if the hard cider is left exposed to oxygen. In an aerobic environment (meaning, exposed to oxygen), the acetobacter begin to take over in the alcoholic environment. Eventually the acetic acid becomes prolific and the beverage becomes apple cider vinegar. This is now primarily an acetic acid fermentation, or vinegar.

At all stages, a culture can be introduced to persuade the microorganisms to go in one direction or another, but if given oxygen, time and warmth, all sugar-containing liquids will go down a similar path.

All of these forms have their health and sustainability benefits. Hard cider, for instance, is generally what you would bottle in order to preserve the apple harvest for long-term storage. Once capped, it can keep for months or years, as would apple cider vinegar. The soft cider is a short-term storage solution, which most "soft" lactic acid–fermented beverages really are.

WILD FERMENTED VS. CULTURED BEVERAGES

There are generally two types of lacto-fermented beverages. The first is the cultured variety in which you add a mother culture—such as kombucha or water kefir—to ferment sweetened water. The second is a wild fermentation, which involves allowing the bacteria present on a raw piece of food to work as the inoculant.

Both have their place, but the beginner is generally more comfortable with something that is more predictable, so cultured beverages are often best to start with. For the more adventurous, you can plunk just about anything containing some sort of bacteria or sugars into a jar of water and it will begin to ferment, but the end result isn't always consistent, nor is it tasty.

KVASS: THE MOTHER OF WILD FERMENTED BEVERAGES

I call these beverages *kvass*. Kvass (or kvas) is actually a traditional beverage from in and around Russia. There are as many types of kvass as there are brewers who make it, but it often was made from day-old bread, sugar, fruits and possibly the addition of a natural yeast. Often made from rye breads, the traditional kvass was a dark, sour, bubbly beverage with a low alcohol content. The end product is not unlike kombucha.

Kvass, however, can be made with pretty much whatever you have on hand that would promote fermentation. Traditionally, it was made as both a tonic and a delicious, home-brewed beverage that families could come together around. And so, you made kvass with what you grew or had in your kitchen.

Today, many kvass recipes call for the inclusion of baker's or brewer's yeast, but this is not necessary nor is it likely traditional. A wild fermentation can be achieved as long as you do the following:

1. Fill the jar ⅓ to ½ full with fruits, veggies, bread or herbs.

2. Always use something that would have bacteria in it—a vegetable, unpeeled fruits, sourdough starter and so forth.

3. Use salt for savory kvasses like beet or cabbage but omit it for sweet kvasses containing fruits and sugars.

The direction you go depends entirely on what you are aiming for. If you desire a strictly utilitarian tonic, salt, beets and cabbage will all make a fine one when added to water. The Carrot-Clementine Kvass (page 191) and the Beet and Apple Kvass (page 185) are both examples of these.

If a sour, bubbly, flavorful and faintly sweet beverage is what you are after, include dried fruits, ginger and sugar. The recipe for Sourdough Bread Kvass (page 167) is an example of this type of kvass. In either case, I make these kvasses with the desire to give our family good bacteria and enzymes. They love them because they are bubbly, taste good and make them feel good. Besides being fun to make, I love these beverages for much the same reason.

Culture Starters in Wild Kvasses

A wild fermentation is generally considered one in which a culture starter is not added. The minute bacteria on the surface of fruits or vegetables simply proliferate in a warm, moist environment, creating a fermented food. Generally speaking, these beverages have a way of working out, but not everyone is comfortable with the concept.

For those who wish to employ a bit more control over their final kvass, there are a few options for culture starters in making fermented beverages. All of these are readily available in a kitchen in which fermentation is a mainstay.

Options for culture starters include:

1. **Sourdough starter.** When you bottle fermented beverages with sourdough starter, a small amount of flour settles to the bottom, much like the dregs of any fermented beverage.

2. **Whey.** This is nearly undetectable in the final product. See page 154 on how to strain cultured dairy and harvest the whey. Most likely because of the yeast content, I find kefir whey to be the most vivacious.

3. **Water kefir and kombucha.** Both of these can be used, just be sure that whatever you choose is freshly but not too strongly fermented, as the acidity can interfere with the natural fermentation process.

Keep in mind with all of these that the bacterial profile of the culture starter will influence the bacterial profile of the final beverage. This isn't necessarily a bad thing, but if you are aiming to diversify the microbes that you intake, wild fermentation is helpful, which is one benefit of its unpredictability.

EQUIPMENT

As for many other fermented foods, the equipment you use in making fermented beverages is simultaneously important and uncomplicated. Here are a few things you'll need to have on hand:

Glass jars. Gallon (4-L) and half-gallon (2-L) jars are going to be more useful here than quarts (1 L), unless you are only fermenting for one person. Larger vessels such as two-gallon (8-L) glass vessels and even custom-made kombucha casks can also be used, though these are rarer. Essentially, you need a large glass vessel to which you can attach a permeable lid using a rubber band.

Permeable lids. Most fermented beverages need to breathe during their first fermentation. The oxygen helps to encourage the yeast population, creating the bubbly beverage we desire. But the sweet liquids that you are fermenting are highly attractive to the ants, fruit flies and other contaminants you do not want in your drinks. For that reason, a clean cloth, a paper towel or a coffee filter fastened with a rubber band or canning ring should be used to cover your jars throughout the fermentation process.

Rubber bands or canning rings. The permeable lids need to be fastened to the jars to keep out fruit flies and other unwanted debris. The best tools for this job are the canning rings that align with the size jar you are using—narrow or wide mouth—or rubber bands of varying sizes.

Funnels. Pouring gallon (4-L) jars of liquid into pint (0.5-L)-size airtight bottles is tricky. Funnels of the correct size and shape are therefore useful in bottling beverages for their second fermentation.

Airtight bottles. The second fermentation can and should produce a fair amount of carbon dioxide to create the carbonation we all love. That same gas can be dangerous if it is not either watched carefully and burped to relieve pressure, or bottled in a vessel designed for such pressure. Both pint (0.5-L) and quart (1-L) jars can be used for a second fermentation, but they will not be able to safely achieve the same level of carbonation as flip-top bottles designed to bottle beer, sodas and all manner of carbonated beverages.

Strainers. Some beverages will need to be strained between the first fermentation and the bottling for the second one. Water kefir and various kvasses all require this step. Having small- to medium-size stainless steel or plastic strainers on hand makes this job quick and painless.

ABOUT THE RECIPES

Passing down food tradition from one generation to the next is often done in the quietest kitchen with only a memory to serve as a recipe. Like these memories, and much of this book, the recipes in this particular chapter are a guide to making delicious wild-fermented kvasses, fermented tonics and cultured probiotic beverages. You can then take these memories and create more with what you have.

Fermented beverages are one of the most delicious and exciting forms of fermented foods, especially for palates unaccustomed to the tang and flavor nuance that fermentation brings to the table. And so many of these recipes are a great starting point or a delicious probiotic secret when served to loved ones. They really taste a lot like a faintly sweet soda.

These include the bubbling, faintly sweet kvasses such as Sweet Potato (page 168), Dried Fruit (page 186), the Pits Soda (page 178) and Sourdough Bread Kvass (page 167). Similarly, the innumerable fruit and herbal flavors make bubbly and faintly sweet Whey Sodas (page 172). These are the beverages that the whole family—the whole community, really—will want to come around.

Other recipes are meant more as a tonic, a digestive aid to be had at or in between meals, a boost in enzymes and probiotics for when you need it most. These are the Cabbage Core Kvass (page 176), Beet and Apple Kvass (page 185) and Carrot and Clementine Kvass (page 191). I make these recipes solely to nourish bellies big and small.

Cultured beverages are mainstays in our kitchen, both for their predictable, self-perpetuating nature and for their flexibility in taking on whatever seasonal fruits we have on the homestead. These are the four gallons (15 L) of Kombucha (page 187) we make every week, the bubbling quarts of Water Kefir (page 181) we love and the Water Kefir Fermented Fruit Juices (page 182) that are crazy delicious. Along with those come a couple of flavoring syrups—Root Beer (page 171) and Ginger Ale (page 177)—that will turn 'buch, water kefir and whey sodas into familiar soft drinks everyone will love.

For something altogether different, I've included a recipe for Fermented Horchata Concentrate (page 175). Since moving closer to the border, I've become familiar with this beverage from Spain and Mexico that is made using altogether different approaches from the kvasses. My recipe uses a rice base, which is fermented using raw honey as both a starter culture and sweetener. Mixed with ice-cold milk, cinnamon and vanilla, it is super-refreshing, sweet and just tangy enough to give away its fermented state.

Once you've grasped the concept of a kvass or the ratio of culture to sweetener, move forward with your own creations. Create your own memories . . . and then share them with the next generation.

Sourdough Bread Kvass

This is what I think of when I think of real kvass. Made from stale bread and whatever sugar or fruits you might have on hand, this bubbly beverage has deep roots. It isn't terribly sweet, nor is it terribly sour. It is not unlike kombucha in that it is both pleasant to drink and good for the belly. Its viscous quality reminds me of a thick beer and its flavor is truly unique and delicious.

Makes: Approximately 3 pints (1.4 L) / Fermentation Time: 5 to 10 days / Storage Time: Several days at room temperature, 1 to 2 weeks in the refrigerator

¼ cup (96 g) sugar

1 cup (237 ml) water, plus more as needed

1 cup (100 g) stale sourdough bread, cubed

1 tsp (7 g) molasses

1 tbsp (5 g) sourdough starter (page 79) or another culture starter, optional

Dissolve the sugar in 1 cup (237 ml) water. Add the sugar water to a quart jar (1 L) along with the sourdough bread cubes and molasses. Stir. Fill the jar with water, leaving 1 inch (25 mm) of headspace. Add the sourdough starter or culture starter if desired.

Seal the jar and leave to ferment for 4 to 8 days, or until tart. Be sure to check the jar daily and burp it as needed to avoid too much pressure in the jar.

Once tangy, strain the kvass from the bread. If carbonation is desired, bottle the decanted kvass in airtight bottles with 1 teaspoon (4 g) sugar per bottle or 2 teaspoons (6 g) of organic raisins. Seal the bottles and allow to ferment an additional 1 to 2 days at room temperature.

Refrigerate or serve over ice. Open bottles carefully, as they may be very carbonated.

Sweet Potato Kvass

Nearly every fall since our arrival in Texas, we have had a sweet potato harvest. Some years have been better than others, but this tuber is a constant in the summer garden. They store really well and bake up nicely when put on a bed of coals in the wood stove. This beverage, however, has changed the game. Often called Sweet Potato Fly, this kvass is sweet and incredibly carbonated—and one of my all-time favorites. A bigger field of sweet potatoes might be in order.

 Makes: Approximately 3 pints (1.4 L) / Fermentation Time: 5 to 9 days / Storage Time: Several days at room temperature, 1 to 2 weeks in the refrigerator

2 cups (360 g) shredded sweet potatoes (1 medium)

¾ cup (144 g) sugar

Water, as needed

Combine the shredded sweet potato and sugar in a half-gallon (2-L) vessel. Fill the rest of the vessel with water, leaving 1 inch (25 mm) of headspace. Cover with a permeable lid such as a coffee filter or clean cloth secured with a rubber band or canning ring.

Set at room temperature to ferment for 3 to 5 days or until it is bubbly and beginning to get tangy. During this time, yeast may accumulate on the surface of the ferment. If it does, you can simply scoop it out. It will abate during the second fermentation.

Once the initial fermentation is underway, strain the sweet potato from the kvass and transfer the liquid to airtight bottles, leaving a bit of headspace, because the carbonation should be strong. Once bottled, leave to ferment at room temperature for at least 2 to 4 days, or until the beverage has a bit of tang and is carbonated.

Consume within a few days if storing at room temperature. Or, refrigerate for 1 to 2 weeks, checking the carbonation frequently to avoid the buildup of too much pressure.

Root Beer Syrup for Any Fermented Drink

Open a bag of dried sassafras root and wintergreen leaf, and you know immediately where they will take you. A decoction begins the journey, boiling all of the flavor and goodness of the roots and seeds into the liquid. Then steep the wintergreen leaves into the decoction to brighten the flavor. Finally, strain and sweeten the syrup, which will last for weeks at room temperature, or for months in the refrigerator. And then, when your kombucha or water kefir is ready for bottling, add a dash of this syrup to sweeten and flavor the second fermentation. Alternatively, this can be mixed with water and whey or with sourdough starter for a root beer soda full of both bubbles and enzymes.

Makes: Approximately 3 cups (710 ml) / Storage Time: 1 month at room temperature, up to 6 months in the refrigerator

3 cups (710 ml) water

½ cup (90 g) sassafras root

1 clove

½ tsp coriander (cilantro) seed

½ tsp ground ginger root

2 tbsp (3 g) broken wintergreen leaves

2½ cups (383 g) sugar

2 tbsp (30 ml) molasses

Make the root decoction: Bring the water to a boil in a small pot. Add the sassafras root, clove, coriander and ginger, and lower the heat. Simmer for 15 minutes.

Steep the tea: Remove the pot from the heat and add the wintergreen leaves. Cover the pot with a lid and leave to steep for 15 more minutes.

Strain and assemble the syrup: Strain the decoction through a fine strainer. Rinse out the pot and return the decoction to the pot. Add the sugar and molasses and bring to a boil. Simmer an additional 5 minutes to concentrate the syrup.

Remove from the heat and allow to cool. Transfer to an airtight container. This syrup will keep for about a month at room temperature, due to the sugar content. It will keep up to 6 months refrigerated.

To serve: Add 1 tablespoon (15 ml) of syrup to a pint (473 ml) of Kombucha (page 187) or Water Kefir (page 181) when you bottle them for the second fermentation. Use ⅓ cup (78 ml) when making Whey Soda (page 172).

How to Make Whey Sodas

One of the simplest fermented beverages to make is a whey soda. It combines the probiotic properties of whey with tasty fruits and sweeteners to create a bubbly drink teeming with good bacteria and enzymes. It is one of the best fermented foods to get skeptics started on. Make fermented fruit juices, lemonades or limeades, ginger ales or fermented herbal teas. All you need is whey and a sweetened liquid.

 Makes: 1 half gallon (1.89 L) / Fermentation Time: 3 to 9 days / Storage Time: Several days at room temperature, 1 to 2 weeks in the refrigerator

USING JUICE

½ gallon (1.9 L) fruit juice

½ cup (118 ml) whey (see page 154)

USING HERBS OR FLAVORINGS

½ gallon (1.9 L) steeped herbal tea or water

¾ cup (144 g) sugar

½ cup (118 ml) whey (see page 154)

Lemon, lime, ginger, etc.

If using juice, simply combine the juice and whey in a half-gallon (2-L) jar. If using sweetened teas or water, steep the tea at a rate of 1 teaspoon (1 g) of herb per cup of water. Strain and add the sugar while still hot. Allow to cool before combining with the whey and other flavorings.

Seal the jar with a lid and allow to ferment for 2 to 6 days, depending on the temperature. Transfer the liquid to airtight bottles for a second fermentation of 1 to 3 days. Pour over ice and consume immediately or transfer to the refrigerator for 1 to 2 weeks.

VARIATIONS: For lemonade, use ½ cup (118 ml) fresh lemon juice with the sugar and water.

For a honey-sweetened version, replace the sugar with ½ cup (118 ml) raw honey.

For root beer, use ⅓ cup (80 ml) of the Root Beer Syrup (page 171) in combination with the sugar, whey and water.

Strain whey from cultured dairy.

Whey should be translucent yellow.

Add whey to fruit juice.

Fermented Horchata Concentrate

Recipes for this drink vary from a chufa-based Spanish beverage to a rice-and-almond-based Mexican version. I found no evidence that this beverage has been traditionally fermented, except maybe the overnight soaking that the rice gets. It is a delicious and refreshing sweet and creamy beverage, so I set out to create a fermented alternative for a bit of a nutritional boost. Here is my version using raw honey as both the sweetener and the starter culture, in a concentrate that is then mixed into almond or dairy milk.

Makes: 2½ to 5 cups (474 to 1,185 ml) concentrate; 2¾ quarts (2,602 ml) finished beverage
Fermentation Time: 4 to 7 days / Storage Time: Up to 1 week at room temperature,
1 to 2 months in the refrigerator

FOR THE CONCENTRATE

1 cup (210 g) white rice

1 cinnamon stick, broken in half

6 cups (1,420 ml) water, divided

½ cup (118 ml) raw honey

TO SERVE

3 cups (710 ml) almond or dairy milk

½ tsp cinnamon

1 tsp (5 ml) vanilla extract

¾ cup (177 ml) concentrate

Combine the rice, cinnamon stick and 4 cups (946 ml) of the water in a medium saucepan. Place over medium heat and bring to a boil. Simmer for 10 minutes and then remove from heat. Stir the additional 2 cups (480 ml) of water into the rice mixture and allow to sit for at least 2 hours or overnight.

Remove the cinnamon stick and either put the rice mixture through a sieve and discard any particles remaining in the sieve, or blend the rice mixture and then strain.

Combine the strained rice mixture with the raw honey in a quart (1 L) jar. Cover with a permeable lid such as a clean cloth or a coffee filter secured with a canning ring or rubber band. Leave to ferment for 4 to 7 days or just until it begins to taste tangy. You may also see hints of bubbles beginning to form. It may separate during the fermentation process. Don't worry if it does; simply stir it all back together again.

Once fermented, this concentrate can be used straight away, stored at room temperature for up to a week (it will get tangier) or refrigerated and stored for 1 to 2 months.

To serve: Combine the milk, cinnamon, vanilla and ¾ cup (180 ml) of the concentrate in a pitcher or quart (1-L) jar. Serve over ice for a refreshing creamy, slightly tangy drink.

Cabbage Core Kvass

Whereas Sweet Potato Kvass (page 168) is intended to be a delightful bubbly beverage that most people will love to imbibe, this is more akin to a tonic. Essentially, it is sauerkraut that is made primarily for the brine. This can be used as a digestive aid, a clean start to the day or even an ingredient in a vinaigrette or smoothie. Besides how good it makes me feel, I love that it essentially creates a probiotic enzyme supplement from the by-product of kraut making.

 Makes: About 3 cups (710 ml) tonic / Fermentation Time: 5 to 10 days / Storage Time: 1 to 2 weeks at room temperature, 1 to 2 months in refrigerator

2 to 4 cabbage cores, or enough to fill a quart (1-L) jar one-third of the way

1 tbsp (15 g) salt

Water as needed

Using the cores left over from making sauerkraut, fill a quart jar one-third of the way with cabbage cores. Add the salt and fill the jar with water, leaving 1 inch (25 mm) of headspace.

Cover with a sealable lid and place out of the way to ferment for at least 5 to 10 days. Check daily to see if the jar needs to be burped. Due to the cabbage's high water content, the fermentation process may proceed more slowly and with less carbonation than a vegetable ferment.

After 5 days, taste. It should be tangy but not overpoweringly so. Continue to ferment if needed. When fermentation is complete, pour off 1 to 2 ounces (30 to 60 ml) to drink as a tonic. Store at room temperature for an additional 1 to 2 weeks or refrigerate for 1 to 2 months.

Ginger Ale Syrup for Any Fermented Drink

Concepts like these beverage syrups are great for keeping everyone interested in fermented beverages. They're a simple one-time effort that produces bottle after bottle of bubbly fermented ginger ale. Just pour a spoonful into kombucha or water kefir on the second fermentation. Or, add a glug to whey soda for that ubiquitous ginger kick. It's really handy stuff.

 Makes: About 2 cups (474 ml) syrup / Storage Time: 1 to 2 weeks at room temperature, 6 to 12 months in refrigerator

1¼ cups (287 g) chopped fresh ginger

2 cups (384 g) sugar

1 cup (237 ml) water

1 tsp (5 ml) vanilla extract

Combine the ginger, sugar and water in a small saucepan. Bring to a boil over high heat and then lower to a simmer. Simmer for 15 minutes to infuse the ginger and create the syrup.

Once the cooking time is up, allow to cool for 10 minutes before handling. Pour the syrup into a pint (0.5-L) jar through a strainer to remove the ginger pieces. Allow to cool completely to room temperature before adding the vanilla and sealing the jar. Shake to mix in the vanilla and then use or store.

Store at room temperature for 1 to 2 months. Refrigerate for 6 to 12 months.

To serve: Add 1 tablespoon (15 ml) of syrup to a pint (473 ml) of Kombucha (page 187) or Water Kefir (page 181) when you bottle for the second fermentation. Use 2 tablespoons (30 ml) when making Whey Soda (page 172).

The Pits Soda

This lively, mellow soda packs a probiotic punch while making use of the castoffs from your summer pie or smoothie. Use pits with a bit of the fruit still clinging to them, and not from fruits that have met the greedy fingers of young children attempting to scrape off every last bit of sweet fruit—while adding their own bit of foreign bacteria.

Makes: 1 pint (474 ml) / Fermentation Time: 2 to 3 days /
Storage Time: 3 to 5 days refrigerated

1 mango pit or ½ cup (75 g) peach, plum, nectarine or another fruit pit

2 tbsp (24 g) sugar

2-3 cups (474-710 ml) water

1 tbsp (15 ml) sourdough starter (page 79), kombucha (page 187), whey (page 154), water kefir (page 181) or another culture starter (optional)

Add the pits to a quart (946 ml) jar along with the sugar, water to fill the jar and the optional culture starter.

Ferment with permeable lid for 2 to 3 days or until bubbles are forming at surface and it looks alive. Strain liquid from pits and transfer to an airtight bottle, cap and allow to ferment an additional 2 to 3 days to carbonate.

Serve over ice, once carbonated. Refrigerate upon carbonation for 3 to 5 days or drink within 48 hours of initial carbonation. Longer room temperature storage can be had by burping bottles twice daily to avoid bottle explosions.

How to Make Water Kefir

The water kefir culture—known as grains—is an insoluble polysaccharide that converts sugar to lactic acid, carbon dioxide and a host of other microorganisms. Essentially it converts sugar water into a probiotic, bubbly drink.

They are akin to milk kefir grains; however, the two cannot be used interchangeably for more than one culturing, as the water kefir grains are not designed to consume milk sugar. They will quickly die and stop converting milk to kefir.

Making water kefir is a simple enough process to easily work into your weekly kitchen routine. The fermentation time is a great deal faster than kombucha, and the flavor is different. While kombucha leans more toward an acetic acid (vinegar) profile, water kefir tends towards alcohol.

Makes: 1 quart (946 ml) / Fermentation Time: 2 to 3 days for first fermentation,
3 to 5 additional days for second fermentation

¼ cup (48 g) sugar

2 tsp (10 ml) molasses, optional

2 cups (474 ml) warm water, more as needed

¼ cup (59 ml) water kefir grains (see below)

Combine the sugar and molasses in a quart (1-L) jar. Pour over the warm water. Stir to dissolve the sugar. Add the water kefir grains and top the jar up with water.

Cover the jar with a permeable lid such as a cloth or coffee filter fastened with a rubber band or canning ring, and place in a warm spot, away from other cultures, to ferment.

Culture the water kefir for approximately 48 hours, depending on the temperature. At this point, the sugar water should be less sweet and have a tangy flavor to it.

Strain the liquid from the grains and transfer to quart jars for storage or airtight bottles for carbonation. Move the grains to a new batch of sugar water and repeat first fermentation for your grains.

To carbonate, add a few fresh fruit slices or 1 to 2 ounces (28 to 57 ml) of fruit juice to the water kefir in airtight bottles. Allow to ferment 3 to 5 days or until bubbly. Drink within two days or refrigerate for 3 to 5 days.

CULTURE CARE: Water kefir grains are the mother culture used in making water kefir. Give the culture the following and the grains will flourish, multiply and produce delicious water kefir:

Warmth. Water kefir grains are one of the most heat-loving cultures. Indeed, in the summer, when it is regularly 100°F (38°C) in our kitchen, water kefir is one of the few cultures I continue on with. Come winter, we keep ferments such as this near our wood stove.

Minerals. Water kefir also performs better in the presence of minerals. Using an unrefined sugar with the minerals still intact is helpful, as is adding molasses and even liquid mineral drops to the fermenting water kefir.

Fermenting Various Fruit Juices
with Water Kefir Grains

One of the most drop-dead delicious fermented beverages I have ever had was a simple fruit juice fermented with water kefir grains. The juice was a cranberry-raspberry mix and, in a matter of two days, the first ferment was finished and I bottled it. Forty-eight hours later, it was bubbly, tangy and unspeakably delicious.

Fruit juice can be fermented with water kefir grains, but only with spare water kefir grains. To ensure that you do not lose your grains by suddenly switching their food source from sugar water to fruit juice, it is safest to simply continue culturing the sugar water while simultaneously using spare kefir grains to culture the fruit juice. The sugars are different in fruit juice than in sugar water–fructose vs. sucrose and glucose, and so forth–therefore the grains may be stressed or even killed from a sudden food switch.

With that said, if you wish to culture fruit juice with water kefir grains, try this method.

 Makes: 1 quart (946 ml) / Fermentation Time: 2 to 3 days

2 tbsp (30 ml) water kefir grains

Scant quart (946 ml) organic fruit juice

Add the grains to the juice. Allow the juice to culture for 2 to 3 days or until bubbly and slightly tangy. Transfer the juice to an airtight container for carbonating. Replenish the grains in sugar water as usual, keeping them separate from your water kefir grains.

If, after a few culturings in sugar water, the grains are performing well, they can be combined with your other water kefir grains or used to culture fruit juice once again.

Beet and Apple Kvass

This riff on the traditional beet kvass is a seasonal marriage of sweet and earthy. A great fall drink, this is my favorite way to do beet kvass. Not too salty, not very sweet and just a little bit tangy—it is a pleasure to drink.

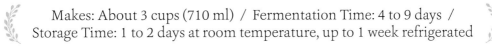

Makes: About 3 cups (710 ml) / Fermentation Time: 4 to 9 days /
Storage Time: 1 to 2 days at room temperature, up to 1 week refrigerated

1 large beet, chopped

1½ large apples, chopped and divided

Water as needed

1 tsp (5 g) sugar, if desired

Combine the beet and 1 of the large apples in a quart (1-L) jar. Fill the jar with water, leaving 1 inch (25 mm) of headspace. Cover and leave to ferment for 3 to 7 days, or until pleasantly tangy.

Strain the kvass from the beet and apple and serve immediately. If carbonation is desired, bottle the kvass with the remaining chopped apple and sugar, if desired. Leave to ferment 1 to 2 more days before consuming or refrigerating.

Dried Fruit Kvass

This simple kvass makes good use of a form of preserved fruit. While fermented fruits do not withstand long-term food storage, they do have a role in lactic acid fermentation in applications such as this. A note of caution: This kvass tends to become very carbonated very quickly, due to the yeasts in the dried fruit. Be very careful opening it and do not let it carbonate for much longer than a day, unless your home is very cool. This kvass can also be utilized to leaven bread (see Fruit Yeasts in the Grains chapter on page 74).

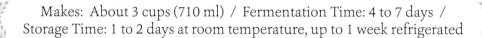

Makes: About 3 cups (710 ml) / Fermentation Time: 4 to 7 days / Storage Time: 1 to 2 days at room temperature, up to 1 week refrigerated

¼ cup (22 g) dried fruit

2 tbsp (24 g) sugar

3 cups (710 ml) water

Combine all ingredients in a quart (1 L) jar. Cover loosely with a lid and set aside to ferment for 3 to 5 days, depending on the temperature. Once it begins to bubble and show other signs of fermentation, decant into an airtight bottle for a bubbly second fermentation of 1 to 2 days. Alternatively, drink it as is over ice for a refreshing kvass.

Vegetable Brine Wellness Shots

Many a time we have turned to fermented vegetable brine to ease tummy aches or give us a bit of energy. The life-giving properties of this liquid are undeniable once you drink it. I find it most potent just after the vegetables have fully fermented (at least 2 weeks). The enzymes and probiotics make us feel lighter almost instantly. This recipe is combines healthful things for a general wellness boost.

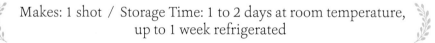

Makes: 1 shot / Storage Time: 1 to 2 days at room temperature, up to 1 week refrigerated

2 tbsp (30 ml) vegetable brine, harvested from any fully fermented vegetable

Pinch of ground turmeric

½ garlic clove, grated

Combine all ingredients in a small glass. Throw it down the hatch and chase with water if needed.

How to Make Kombucha

This ancient fermented tea is beginning to go mainstream—what a great alternative to sugar-laden sodas and drinks! Making it at home, however, costs about 10 percent of what you would pay in a store, which is just one of the reasons you might want to consider this simple brewing practice.

Another reason to consider brewing your own kombucha is that you can tailor it to your tastes, customize the flavor and sweetness, and have as much on hand as you can make. We like to have at least four gallons (15 L) brewing at all times.

Culture care. To ferment kombucha, you use the kombucha SCOBY as the mother culture. Give it the following and it will give you a new SCOBY every time and produce delicious, vibrant kombucha:

Air. Kombucha uses a heavily aerobic fermentation process. The acetobacter, which produce the acetic acid, love oxygen, as do the yeasts in the culture. Using a vessel with a wide-open lid is helpful as it increases the surface area that is exposed to oxygen.

Moderate warmth. Kombucha's fermentation time depends on the temperature at which it is fermented. Too cool and the fermentation takes an inordinate amount of time, which stresses the culture. Too warm and the fermentation happens too rapidly, which also stresses the culture. Strive for a temperature of 70 to 90°F (21 to 32°C) if at all possible.

 Makes: 1 gallon (3.8 L) / Fermentation Time: 1 to 2 weeks for initial fermentation, an additional 3 to 7 days for the second fermentation

FIRST FERMENTATION

8 cups (1.8 L) water, divided

8 tea bags or loose tea leaf equivalent

1 cup (192 g) sugar

1 kombucha SCOBY

1 cup (237 ml) previously brewed kombucha

SECOND FERMENTATION

Scant pint (473 ml) freshly fermented kombucha

A few pieces of fresh fruit, or 2 to 3 ounces (55 to 85 ml) fruit juice

FIRST FERMENTATION

Bring 4 cups (946 ml) of water to a boil over high heat. While the water is heating, place the tea bags and sugar in a ½-gallon (2-L) vessel. Pour the hot water into the jar and allow the tea to brew for 3 to 5 minutes. Remove the tea bags and stir the sugar into the tea to dissolve.

Fill the jar the remainder of the way with cold filtered water. Let the tea cool to body temperature. Test the temperature by inserting a clean finger into it. If you can hold your finger in without burning, the tea is cool enough to use.

To a 1-gallon (4-L) glass jar, add the body-temperature tea, SCOBY and previously brewed kombucha. Top the jar up the remainder of the way with filtered water. Cover the jar with a clean towel, cloth or coffee filter, and secure it with a rubber band.

Place the jar in a warm space, out of direct sunlight and away from other aerobic cultures such as sourdough and milk kefir. Allow to ferment for 1 to 2 weeks or until a new baby SCOBY has formed on the surface and the kombucha tastes at least a bit tangy.

(continued)

How to Make Kombucha (continued)

The fermentation time will vary, depending on the temperature at which you are brewing and the size of the vessel you are using. Kombucha loves oxygen, so a wider jar opening seems to help it along in the brewing process.

With that said, you do not want your kombucha to brew too fast. Like all fermented foods, it needs to strike a balance, as different bacteria and yeasts thrive under different conditions. If the culture experiences extremes of temperature, it can be stressed and begin to produce "off" batches. In general, a moderate temperature of 65 to 85°F (18 to 29°C) is recommended.

The kombucha is done when the taste is just right for your palate, so long as it is tangy and a SCOBY has formed. If, however, you wish to bottle and carbonate your kombucha, you should do so when it is tangy but still fairly sweet, because sugar produces carbonation.

When it is done, or when you are ready to bottle it, drink it as is or pour the kombucha off into a separate vessel to refrigerate, or drink it over the course of several days. Leave the kombucha SCOBY and at least 1 cup (237 ml) of the fermented kombucha in the vessel and repeat the brewing instructions above, adding the cooled, sweetened tea to the SCOBY and proceeding with brewing as before.

What is a SCOBY?

The mother culture for making kombucha is called a SCOBY. This stands for symbiotic colony of bacteria and yeast. It is not, as is often thought, a mushroom. Rather it is the result of the growth of acetobacter as is proven by the presence of a similarly structured organism forming in the making of homemade vinegars or acetic acid bacteria-containing beverages. The shape and size of the SCOBY is determined by the vessel in which the kombucha is brewed as it will grow on the surface of the kombucha, starting as a very thin film, and will eventually fill the vessel with a gelatinous disc.

What to Do With All of Those SCOBYs

Every time kombucha is properly fermented, the mother culture creates a baby SCOBY. You will see it as a light film on top of the kombucha at first. By the time the fermentation is done, it will appear as a full SCOBY, thick enough to remove and use to create another batch of kombucha.

If you are not inclined to start another batch of kombucha, you will quickly amass a great deal of SCOBYs. It is a myth that the more SCOBYs your kombucha has, the faster it will ferment. So you will need to find a use for those SCOBYs.

If you want to save them to give to friends, you can start a SCOBY hotel simply by placing them in a jar and covering them with kombucha. You can then add to the hotel when needed. Then remove one and give it to a friend, along with a cup (237 ml) of fermented kombucha, when they want to start brewing their own.

Kombucha SCOBYs can also be chopped and dehydrated for animal jerky, chopped and given to chickens or pigs, or simply thrown into the compost pile to add a bit of bacteria to your fermenting compost.

SECOND FERMENTATION

If you want to achieve a fizzy, flavored kombucha like the kind you can purchase, you need to bottle the kombucha separate from the SCOBY and add fruits or juices as desired. As the fermented kombucha consumes the residual or added sugars, carbon dioxide is produced, which carbonates the drink.

Note that you need to carefully choose your bottling vessels, as eventually the gases will build to the point of being dangerous. Jars and bottles not designed to hold carbonated beverages can crack or even explode. So choose flip-top bottles, bottles used for commercially-made kombucha or German Grolsch bottles for your second fermentation.

You can flavor kombucha with just about any fruit, juice or flavoring. Either a few slices of whatever seasonal fruit you have on hand or a little bottled juice work well. If you desire a crisp, plain kombucha with no added flavorings, bottle it when it is still pretty sweet, or simply add 1 teaspoon (4 g) of sugar to the bottles.

Add the fruit or juice to your bottle and cover with kombucha, leaving a bit of headspace for carbonation. Tightly fasten the lid and leave the kombucha to ferment at room temperature for several days or until bubbly. Consume within 1 to 2 days to avoid overcarbonation, or store in the refrigerator for 1 to 2 weeks.

Make Kombucha Vinegar!

Kombucha, more than many other lacto-fermented foods, contains a great deal of acetic acid. The predominant acid in vinegar, acetic acid becomes more and more prolific throughout the kombucha brewing process. If you allow the kombucha's first fermentation to go on at least a week or two beyond the stage at which you would harvest it for drinking, you end up with essentially kombucha vinegar. This may not have quite the acidity of vinegar (which is often 5 to 6 percent), but it is tangy enough to be used as a vinegar substitute in salad dressings and other recipes. This is just one more way to save money and make the most of what you already have.

Carrot-Clementine Kvass

This is a choose-your-own-adventure kvass. The carrot lends the bacteria, and the clementines add some delicious flavor. Add sugar to the first ferment for a sweeter, bubblier kvass. Add sugar only to the second fermentation for a tangy, slightly bubbly kvass. Omit the sugar altogether for something akin to a tangy tonic.

 Makes: Approximately 3 cups (710 ml) / Fermentation Time: 4 to 8 days / Storage Time: Several days at room temperature, 1 to 2 weeks in the refrigerator

1 large carrot, cut into 1-inch (25 mm) chunks

3 clementines, peeled

¼ cup (48 g) sugar (optional), plus an additional 2 tsp (8 g), divided

Water

Combine the carrot and clementines in a quart (1-L) jar, adding the sugar, if a sweet kvass is desired. Add water, leaving 1 inch (25 mm) of headspace from the lip of jar.

Cover with a porous cloth or coffee filter and secure with a rubber band or canning ring.

Leave to ferment at room temperature for 3 to 6 days, or until very bubbly and aromatic. Transfer to an airtight bottle, add the remaining 2 teaspoons (8 g) sugar and cap. Leave to ferment for an additional 1 to 2 days before serving or refrigerating.

Condiments

Sauces and condiments are often the glue that brings humble ingredients together. With these at the table, you can eat simple vegetables, proteins and grains day in and day out, without ever feeling deprived. When that desire for the exciting restaurant food creeps in, these little jars provide everything we want right at home, with wholesome ingredients.

The more committed we have become to homemade or homegrown, the more desirous I have become of a dynamic collection of recipes for preserving and preparing what we are given.

Tangy, salty, flavorful recipes such as these can sit on the table for weeks, bringing inspiration to a meal that might otherwise be wanting.

And everyone—big or small—likes to dip, dunk and splash their food to their liking, I find. If a jar filled with good things brings everyone to the table and nourishes them in the process, then what more can a family cook want?

THE SUSTAINABLE SIDE OF FERMENTED CONDIMENTS

For die-hard homesteaders, it may seem frivolous to go to the trouble of making condiments when simple fare is work enough to get on the table. I hear you. Most of our meals are simple one-pan affairs with a ferment and whatever seasonal vegetables we happen to have. But still, I make fermented condiments not just because they are delicious, but also because they promote sustainability at the dinner table by:

Making just about anything you happen to have on hand taste awesome. Beans, potatoes, eggs, grains and vegetables can all seem bland and boring. But they are easy to grow or cheap to procure, so it is imperative that we be able to eat these foods meal after meal. These fermented condiments bring excitement to these staple foods.

Turning simple homestead ingredients into preserved sauces. Real Louisiana Hot Sauce is traditionally made by fermenting peppers for weeks or months, and then blending them into a fermented sauce with a depth of flavor unmatched by common methods. This method of fermenting the peppers whole preserves them, so when you blend the sauce, it is also well preserved. Making salsas and sauces from what you glean is just another way to make the most of what you have.

Replacing the need to purchase their commercial counterparts. Even when you must buy things like yogurt or salsa ingredients at the store, you will still be saving a great deal of money on store-bought condiments by making them at home.

Packing enzymes and probiotics. If eating fermented foods every day or at every meal is your goal, fermented condiments give you one more way in which to add a little bit here and a little bit there. Using cultured salad dressing at lunch and fermented hot sauce on supper tacos go a long way toward these goals of saving money while eating traditionally and sustainably.

FOOD PRESERVATION AND FERMENTED CONDIMENTS

I believe it is a myth that all condiments were once fermented. Some of them certainly were, but others were preserved without canning or refrigeration by the simple addition of vinegar, sugar and spices, all of which prevent bacterial growth from taking place.

In making fermented condiments, we want (good) bacterial growth. We want naturally occurring bacteria on the vegetables or fruit to take hold and proliferate, producing lactic acid and preventing further (undesirable) bacteria from taking hold.

Some fermented condiments are preserved via their fermentation, while others simply combine a few fermented foods to make an enzymatic and tasty addition to your meal. Some fermented condiments are a slurry of foods combined and then fermented, while others are fermented whole and then whizzed into a probiotic slurry.

If your aim is long-term food preservation, your best bet is to ferment the vegetables whole for weeks or months before combining and blending them into a fermented condiment. The second-best option is to make a roughly chopped salsa that you can submerge below the level of a brine in order to keep it in an anaerobic state.

Smooth, blended hot sauces, salsas and ketchups are all difficult to preserve for longer periods because the brine emulsifies into the foods—tomatoes, peppers and so forth—that you are trying to ferment. For that reason, I recommend you use these blended condiments for short-term storage, table enjoyment and health, rather than storing them for the long term.

ABOUT THE RECIPES

Condiments are meant to liven up and add flavor to those foods that are often thought of as mundane. I specifically designed the recipes in this chapter for those who want to use ferments they already have on hand or those who want to ferment their abundance into something altogether unique and delicious.

Simply preserve Whole Fermented Tomatoes (page 60) in a salt brine when you are crunched for time, and then blend them into a delicious Fermented Marinara (page 214) after months in the root cellar.

Take that basket from the farmer's market when peppers, tomatoes and onions are all at their peak and make a fresh Fermented Garden Salsa (page 202) that will last for months in cold storage. Or use vegetable brine from the many batches of pickles you've made and turn it into Veg Brine Fermented Hot Sauce (page 198), Veg Brine Homestead Fermented Herb Sauce (page 217) and even Veg Brine Mayonnaise (page 205).

If you are after something a little different, use honey to ferment a piquant Fermented Zucchini and Mostarda (page 209) filled with tons of flavor and seasonal produce. Or combine tangy tomatillos with charred onions for a fermented salsa with a unique flavor. Finally, if you miss the condiments of your childhood, Fermented Ketchup (page 213) and Cultured Dairy Ranch Dressing (page 210) will bring you back.

Let these recipes guide you, with the aid of fermentation, toward wholesome jars filled with garden and orchard bounty and meals filled with your favorite fermented ingredients.

Charred Onion Tomatillo Salsa

While tomatoes struggle along in our hot, dry summers, tomatillos seem to thrive. This salsa is an example of our "don't fight it; eat it" take on food production. Pairing fresh tomatillos with garlic, cilantro and lime seems only natural. Adding a bit of charred onion turns this fresh salsa into something pretty spectacular.

 Makes: Approximately 3 cups (720 ml) / Fermentation Time: 1 to 3 weeks / Storage Time: Up to 6 to 12 months

1 large sweet onion

1 ¼ lb (560 g) tomatillos, chopped finely

2 large garlic cloves, minced

⅓ cup (80 g), loosely packed, cilantro

Scant 1 tbsp (15 g) sea salt

Juice of 1 lime

1 jalapeño, seeded and diced, or ¼ tsp red pepper flakes

Water to cover

Char the onion whole over an open flame on the stove and then dice. Alternatively, dice the onion and place in a dry cast-iron or stainless steel skillet with no oil or water. Place the skillet over low heat and cook 8 to 10 minutes, stirring occasionally, until the onion turns a dark, almost burnt brown. Remove from heat and allow to cool to room temperature.

Meanwhile, dice the tomatillos finely and add them to a medium-size mixing bowl. Add the garlic, cilantro, salt, lime and jalapeño or pepper flakes. If you taste the salsa at this point, it will be tangy and just a bit salty, which is what we want.

Once the onions have cooled completely, add them to the tomatillo mixture and stir to combine. Transfer the salsa to a quart (1-L) jar, along with any liquid that remains in the bottom of the bowl. Press the salsa down with the back of a spoon to below the level of its own brine. There will not be much brine initially, so add a couple of heavy fermentation weights to keep the salsa weighted down. After a day in the salt, the amount of brine will have increased as moisture is drawn out of the vegetables.

Cover the jar tightly and allow to ferment for at least a week at warm room temperature or up to 3 weeks at cooler room temperature (65 to 75°F [18 to 24°C]). Transfer to cold storage.

VARIATION: Fermenting salsas can be challenging because of the tiny bits and pieces that tend to bob above the brine, bringing unwanted spoilage during cold storage. To avoid this, consider fermenting all of the vegetables except the charred onions in a simple brine solution. Chop the tomatillos just small enough to fit through the mouth of a jar. Add whole-leaf cilantro and whole garlic cloves, a small whole jalapeño and a peeled whole lime. Make a brine by combining 2½ tablespoons (38 g) of salt with 1 quart (946 ml) of water. Pour over as much brine as is needed to cover vegetables. Weigh them down so that the brine covers the vegetables by at least an inch. Cover and allow to ferment for at least 3 weeks. When you want salsa, simply remove all ingredients except the brine and chop or blend. Taste for salt and adjust the seasoning.

Veg Brine Fermented Hot Sauce

Our family really likes hot sauce, and I really like to avoid food waste. The vegetable brine left over from a batch of brine-fermented veggies can be used to make all sorts of delicious probiotic-rich sauces and snacks; this is one of them. For an authentic hot sauce that preserves the pepper harvest, see Whole Fermented Peppers and Sauce on page 59. For a way to turn your overly tangy fermented salsa into a hot sauce, see Overfermented Salsa Hot Sauce (page 206).

 Makes: Approximately 1½ cups (360 ml) / Storage Time: 1 to 2 months

1 garlic clove

1 cup (237 ml) vegetable brine

2 tsp (5 g) ground cayenne pepper

2½ tbsp (37 ml) tomato paste

1–2 tbsp (15–30 ml) raw apple cider vinegar, if necessary

Salt, if needed

Combine garlic, brine, cayenne pepper and tomato paste in a medium bowl. Whisk to combine and taste for salt and acidity. Add apple cider vinegar 1 tablespoon (15 ml) at a time until the sauce is tangy enough. Only add salt if needed, as the brine should be pretty salty.

Transfer to a hot sauce dispenser and leave on the table to enjoy for 2 to 3 weeks. Refrigerate after a week at room temperature for a storage time of 1 to 2 months. The hot sauce may separate during this time, so simply shake it to reblend.

Fermented Pear and Ginger Sauce

Although not appropriate for long-term food storage, recipes like these are great when you need to use up an abundance of fruit and extend its shelf life for just another week. The zingy combination of lactic acid fermentation and ginger makes this sauce irresistible. I recommend mixing it half-and-half with milk kefir for the most delicious natural energy drink.

 Makes: Approximately 2 quarts (1.9 L) / Fermentation Time: 1 to 3 days / Storage Time: Up to 1 week in the refrigerator

12 very ripe pears

1 thumb-size piece of ginger

½ cup (118 ml) kombucha or water kefir, or ¼ cup (59 ml) whey

Blend the pears or push them through a sieve or food mill to make a rough purée.

Grate in the ginger and add the fermentation liquid. Mix together thoroughly and transfer to quart (1-L) jars. Cover and allow to ferment on the counter for 1 to 3 days, depending on the temperature. They are done when they begin to bubble, and the flavor is slightly carbonated and both tangy and sweet. The top may brown a bit from oxidation. This can simply be stirred in and is perfectly fine.

Transfer to the refrigerator or consume at once. Will keep in the refrigerator for up to a week.

Use as a topping for porridge or pancakes, mixed into yogurt or kefir, or to top ice cream.

Fermented Garden Salsa

For those who love the fresh flavors of pico de gallo, this is your salsa. Combining fresh ingredients from the garden when they are at their peak gives this salsa its flavor. Fermenting lends to the salsa organic acids and their undeniable punch. It is tangy, fresh, refreshing and highly enzymatic. Feel free to use whatever produce you might have on hand for this one. Just don't skimp on the onions, cilantro and garlic!

Makes: 2 quarts (1.9 L) / Fermentation Time: 1 to 2 weeks /
Storage Time: 2 to 6 weeks at room temperature, 2 to 6 months refrigerated

1 large red or yellow onion, or a large bunch of green onions

3 small bell peppers, trimmed and cored

6 large garlic cloves, peeled and minced

½ cup (20 g) cilantro leaves, packed

2½ lb (1.1 kg) roma tomatoes, cut into quarters

Juice of 1 lemon

3 tbsp (45 g) sea salt

¼–½ tsp cayenne powder

Chop the onions, bell peppers, garlic, cilantro and tomatoes and combine in a large mixing bowl. Add the lemon juice, salt and cayenne and mix all the ingredients together with a wooden spoon. Taste the salsa for heat and salt. Add more cayenne or salt if the salsa tastes bland. It should taste just a little bit salty; the flavor will mellow through the fermentation period.

Transfer the salsa to 2 quart (1-L)-size jars or 1 half-gallon (2-L) jar. Use a fermentation weight (page 33) to weigh the vegetables down. Cover tightly with a lid and place in a warm spot to ferment for 1 to 2 weeks, burping the jars twice daily for the first week. During this period, the pieces of the vegetables will release a fair amount of their juice and separate a bit. You can give the salsa a quick stir and add more weights to further submerge the vegetables.

Once the salsa is tangy, bubbly and well-fermented, transfer to cold storage or use within 2 to 4 weeks.

Veg Brine Mayonnaise

Mayonnaise is another example of a food I see no reason to ferment—it is an emulsification of oil and acid using egg yolk as the catalyst. To add a culture starter to something that is primarily a fat makes no sense to me. I do, however, see a reason to use vegetable brine in place of the acid to lend enzymes and create a creamy, delicious spread with a product that is underappreciated, in my opinion.

This mayonnaise is a bit thinner than the customary store-bought version when it is first prepared. Chilling it for at least a couple of hours thickens it up, as does using olive oil for at least 25 percent of the oil.

 Makes: Approximately 1½ cups (360 ml) / Storage Time: 1 week

3 egg yolks

2 tbsp (30 ml) fermented vegetable brine, harvested from any fully fermented vegetables

½ tbsp (7 ml) raw apple cider vinegar

1 tbsp (7 ml) prepared Dijon mustard

¼ tsp sea salt

1 cup (237 ml) olive, sunflower, avocado or grapeseed oil (or a combination)

Whisk together the egg yolks, vegetable brine, apple cider vinegar, mustard and salt in a medium bowl.

Using a whisk, slowly drizzle the oil into the egg yolk mixture 1 drop at a time while whisking constantly. Gradually increase the speed of the oil drizzle until it is a continuous thin stream, all while whisking constantly to emulsify. Continue whisking until all of the oil has been added and the mayonnaise is completely emulsified.

Transfer to a serving dish to serve straight away or refrigerate and consume within 1 week.

Overfermented Salsa Hot Sauce

In the gripping Texas heat of August, I only make vegetable ferments that we will eat within a couple of weeks… unless I forget about them. On one such occasion, I left a jar of salsa a bit too long and come September I popped it open. It was delicious, but so incredibly tangy it was almost hard to eat. Because of the high temperatures, it was also quite mushy.

It was from that jar that this recipe was born, a sauce my husband dubbed his favorite as he poured more onto his tacos with tears running down his cheeks.

Makes: 2 cups (474 ml) / Storage Time: 2 to 3 weeks on the counter, 1 to 2 months refrigerated

1 pint (473 ml) Fermented Garden Salsa (page 202)

1–2 tsp (3–5 g) ground cayenne, or to taste

2 tsp (10 ml) apple cider vinegar, or more if your salsa isn't terribly tangy

Salt, if needed

Liquidize the salsa by putting it through a sieve or food mill or blending. Combine liquidized salsa with cayenne and vinegar in a pint (0.5-L)-size jar. Put a lid on the jar and shake very well for 1 to 2 minutes to combine all ingredients. Taste and add more vinegar, cayenne or salt to taste, keeping in mind that the cayenne will be more pronounced after the sauce has time to sit.

Dispense into a hot sauce bottle with an airtight lid or store in the pint jar. Serve immediately, keep at room temperature for 2 to 3 weeks, or refrigerate for 1 to 2 months.

VARIATIONS: Got overfermented, mushy cucumber pickles? Make a relish by chopping the cucumbers finely.

Got overfermented, mushy kraut? Put it through a food mill or blender with equal parts olive oil for a salad dressing.

Got overfermented green beans or carrots? Chop or blend with fresh herbs and garlic for a sauce that will go with any protein, salad or roasted vegetable.

Fermented Zucchini and Fruit Mostarda

A mostarda is an Italian fruit and mustard condiment often made with wine. As such, it's meant to be just a touch boozy. Fermenting fruit in combination with the ever-prolific zucchini creates a tangy, sweet, pungent condiment perfect for pairing with rich charcuterie or fresh and aged cheeses. Note that you must use raw honey as it provides bacteria.

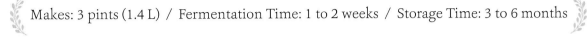

Makes: 3 pints (1.4 L) / Fermentation Time: 1 to 2 weeks / Storage Time: 3 to 6 months

4 cups (600 g) chopped zucchini, 2 medium

4 cups (600 g) chopped hard apple or pear

¼ cup (40 g) chopped dried fruit

3 tbsp (30 g) whole yellow mustard seed

6 tbsp (89 ml) raw honey

1 tbsp (15 g) salt

2 tsp (5 g) ground mustard

Combine all ingredients in a large bowl and mix thoroughly to combine.

Transfer to 3 pint (0.5-L) jars or 1 quart (1-L) plus 1 pint jar. Use a fermentation lid to weigh down the mostarda and seal the jars.

Place the jars at room temperature to ferment for 1 to 2 weeks. Check the jars daily during this period and burp as necessary. Transfer to cold storage where the mostarda will keep for 3 to 6 months, depending on your storage temperature and conditions.

Serve with rich meats, cheeses, sourdough bread and crackers.

Cultured Dairy Ranch Dressing

This creamy, fresh and lively staple dressing can be made from any cultured dairy you happen to have on hand. It's simple to mix up a large batch and keep for salads or dips throughout the week. You won't believe how delicious the homemade version can be!

 Makes: Approximately 2 cups (480 ml) / Storage Time: Up to one week

1 cup (237 ml) sour cream (page 159)

¾ cup (177 ml) buttermilk (page 159), kefir (page 125) or yogurt (page 127)

¼ cup (59 ml) Brine Mayonnaise (page 205)

1 tbsp (15 ml) freshly squeezed lemon juice

½ tsp onion powder or 2 tbsp (6 g) minced green onions

¼ cup (10 g), packed finely chopped fresh parsley

1 tsp (1 g) fresh dill or ¼ tsp dried

1 tsp (5 g) sea salt, or to taste

¼ tsp black pepper

Combine all ingredients in a quart (1-L) jar. Fasten the lid tightly and shake for 1 to 2 minutes to blend. Let rest for at least 15 minutes before serving to allow flavors to meld. Serve as a dip with raw veggies or pour over a fresh green salad.

Store in the refrigerator for up to a week or use up within 1 to 2 days.

VARIATIONS: Use 2 cups (480 ml) total of any cultured dairy you have on hand, considering the richness that sour cream and mayonnaise lend. If sour cream is omitted, use 1 cup (237 ml) of strained yogurt (page 121) and 1 cup (237 ml) of buttermilk, kefir or plain yogurt.

Fermented Ketchup, Two Ways

The ubiquitous condiment gets a fermented makeover in this recipe, using whatever you have on hand. Both versions are made from simple homemade or store-bought tomato paste. The main difference in these two methods is that one is fermented by adding a small quantity of some type of starter culture. The other, quicker, method involves mixing in a large quantity of fermented liquid—kombucha or water kefir—to act as culture, sweetener and acid. All ways are delicious.

 Makes: Scant 2 cups (474 ml) / Fermentation Time: 3 to 10 days / Storage Time: 2 to 4 weeks

CULTURED KETCHUP

6 oz (170 g) tomato paste

4 tbsp (59 ml) whey (page 154), kombucha (page 187) or water kefir (page 181), divided

¼ cup (60 ml) raw apple cider vinegar

⅛ tsp ground cayenne

⅛ tsp ground black pepper

⅛ tsp ground cinnamon

⅛ tsp ground cloves

¾ tsp salt

5 tbsp (75 ml) raw honey

¼ cup (60 ml) of water, or more to reach desired consistency

QUICK "CULTURED" KETCHUP

6 oz (170 g) tomato paste

½ cup (118 ml) kombucha (page 154) or water kefir (page 181)

2 tbsp (30 ml) raw apple cider vinegar

⅛ tsp ground cayenne

⅛ tsp ground black pepper

⅛ tsp ground cinnamon

⅛ tsp ground cloves

¾ tsp salt

4 tbsp (60 ml) raw honey

CULTURED KETCHUP

Combine the tomato paste, 2 tablespoons (30 ml) of whey, vinegar, cayenne, pepper, cinnamon, cloves, salt, honey and water in a small bowl. Whisk well to combine, adding more water as needed for a thinner ketchup. Transfer to a small jar, packing the ketchup down and allowing any liquid to rise above the paste. Add the remaining 2 tablespoons (30 ml) of fermentation liquid to the jar to cover the ketchup and seal the jar.

Leave to ferment for 3 to 10 days, tasting after the first 3 days for tang. Allow to ferment until tangy and fermented, or to taste. Consume within 2 weeks or refrigerate for up to a month.

QUICK "CULTURED" KETCHUP

Whisk all ingredients well until completely combined. Taste and adjust salt and vinegar if needed. Serve immediately.

Raw Fermented Marinara Sauce

In the deep of winter, there is nothing like pulling a jar from the pantry that brings back memories of sunshine on dew-kissed red tomatoes. This recipe does just that, with a little windowsill basil and garlic from the pantry added. The flavor and freshness brought forth through the fermented tomatoes makes this marinara one of the best we've ever had. And I love that it creates something insanely delicious using one of the easiest of food preservation methods—throwing tomatoes in a salt brine so you can get back to the rest of the harvest.

 Makes: About 2 cups (474 ml) marinara / Storage Time: Several days at room temperature, up to 2 weeks in the refrigerator

1 batch whole fermented tomatoes (page 60), 1 lb (0.45 kg)

4 large fresh basil leaves

1 garlic clove

Brine from the fermented tomatoes, as needed for blending

Salt to taste, if needed

Blend tomatoes either by pushing through a sieve or food mill or by using a blender. Add brine from the fermented tomatoes, only as needed, to liquefy the tomatoes in the blender.

Mince the basil and garlic and add to the tomato sauce. Taste for salt and add just a pinch more seasoning, if necessary.

Serve this marinara over zucchini noodles for a fully raw pasta or, if you're preserving tomatoes by the gallon through fermentation, triple or quadruple this recipe for a crowd and serve over warm pasta.

Keeps at room temperature for a few days but watch for surface yeasts. Will keep in the refrigerator for a couple of weeks.

Veg Brine Homestead Fermented Herb Sauce

There is a reason sauces like this—the chimichurri of Argentina, the pesto sauce of Italy—exist in countries in which ties to the ancient food culture run deep. A handful of your potted herbs, a splash of acidity, a hit of spice are everything you need to create a sauce that will dress up literally anything. This version happens to use the brine from fermented vegetables as the acidic component. If you are looking to preserve some herbs, this sauce will do so but only for several weeks at room temperature and a couple of months in the refrigerator. For longer herb storage, see Fermented Fresh Herbs (page 42).

 Makes: About 1½ cups (355 ml) sauce / Fermentation Time: Up to 2 weeks / Storage Time: 2 weeks at room temperature, up to 2 months in the refrigerator

1¼ cups (50 g), tightly packed, fresh herbs (cilantro, parsley, basil, thyme, oregano)

½ cup (118 ml) tangy vegetable brine left over from a batch of fermented vegetables

2 garlic cloves, minced

¼ tsp red pepper flakes

Salt to taste

For a roughly chopped sauce, finely mince the herbs and then combine with all other ingredients with a mortar and pestle. Pound the sauce to break up the herbs and combine the different components into a rough slurry. Alternatively, blend all ingredients in a blender until smooth.

Transfer to a pint (0.5-L) jar and allow sauce to sit for at least several hours for the flavors to meld. The vegetable brine will begin to ferment the herbs. Leave to ferment for up to 2 weeks. Can be stored at room temperature for up to 2 weeks. Will keep in the refrigerator for 1 to 2 months.

Resources

CULTURES

Cultures for Health (culturesforhealth.com): Dehydrated yogurt, kefir, sourdough, water kefir and kombucha starter cultures and more.

Yemoos (yemoos.com): Primarily water and milk kefir grains.

Cutting Edge Cultures (cuttingedgecultures.com): Vegetable culture starter and kefir starter culture.

Kombucha Kamp (kombuchakamp.com): Fresh kombucha SCOBYs.

Azure Standard (azurestandard.com): This U.S.-based, nationwide food co-op now carries several types of culture starters.

EQUIPMENT

Cultures for Health: Almost anything you need to ferment vegetables, grains, dairy, beverages and condiments. Also carries a line of wine and beer fermentation equipment, as well as cheesemaking items such as butter muslin, cheesecloth, cheese molds, rennet and mesophilic cheese cultures.

Amazon: Jars, airlocks, strainers, funnels, bottles and more can all be found at this one-stop online shop.

Local Hardware Stores: These are a great source for pint (0.5-L), quart (1-L) and half-gallon (2-L) jars. You can also find funnels, strainers and other kitchen equipment at reasonable prices.

INGREDIENTS

Flour and Sugar

Tropical Traditions (tropicaltraditions.com): This company carries a great line of flours and sugars that have been tested for glyphosate.

Azure Standard: This U.S.-based, nationwide food co-op carries organic wheat and gluten-free flours in bulk at reasonable prices. You can also purchase sucanat, organic cane sugar and coconut sugar for making fermented beverages.

Local Produce and Dairy

Local Harvest (localharvest.org): This website will get you in touch with local farmers and farmer's markets to find the freshest, most delicious vegetables and fruits for fermentation.

A Campaign for Real Milk (realmilk.com): This website will help you find local farmers producing fresh, raw milk for making clabber and other raw or cultured milk products.

Further Reading

100% Rye by Shannon Stonger

Nourishing Traditions by Sally Fallon

The Nourished Kitchen by Jennifer McGruther

Cultured Food Life by Donna Schwenk

The Art of Natural Cheesemaking by David Asher

Dom's About Kefir (http://users.sa.chariot.net.au/~dna/kefirpage.html): A website dedicated to kefir, its history and lore, and its usefulness and medicinal and culinary application.

Nourishing Days (nourishingdays.com): The author's blog, which details her family's pursuit of agrarianism and the traditional food recipes they make along the way.

Traditional Cooking School (traditionalcookingschool.com)

Acknowledgments

I don't believe in coincidences. When my editor emailed me two weeks after I had our fifth baby, I had to laugh. I had no clue how, given the timing, I could write this cookbook. But my prayer throughout was that the Lord would take it away if that was His will, or make it happen if that was His will.

And here we are.

This book would not be what it is if it weren't for my editor Elizabeth, who tirelessly answered questions and acted as a long-suffering sounding board in many an email. And thanks to my publisher Will, for taking the time to find out what mattered to me and partnering with me to bring it to fruition.

I believe there is nothing new under the sun, so I would like to thank the many authors and recipe-scratchers throughout time from whom I have gleaned. Your words and recipes inspired this book, but even more so, you have inspired the nourishment of my own children. There are no words for how valuable that has been to us.

To the Cultures for Health team for their continuing partnership and support and for providing the many culturing supplies you see in this book. I'd especially like to thank Julie for her loyalty and friendship to our family.

To my family and friends who, no matter the distance, have always been there.

To those in our community: You have walked alongside us, shared our joys and our struggles and, most significantly, have prayed for us. Thank you.

This book literally could not have happened if it weren't for my husband, Stewart. You made this book possible by immersing yourself in the most unpretentious tasks of everyday parenthood. Thank you for your love and service to our family. We love you.

To Elijah, Abram, Annabelle, Ruthie and baby Joshua. You were alongside me in the kitchen, on my hip at the camera and in the pasture with Daddy when Mama had to write. This book was *our* work. But you ... you are my first ministry; my most precious earthly gifts.

And because I have no better words, I must quote A.W. Pink from a book whose fateful prose changed my life:

"If the reader has received blessing from the perusal of these pages, let him not fail to return thanks to the Giver of every good and every perfect gift, ascribing all praise to His inimitable and sovereign grace."

—The Sovereignty of God

About the Author

Shannon Stonger has been fascinated with the inner workings of fermented foods for over a decade. With five young children at home and a passion for sustainability, she has found these foods to be both a necessity and a blessing.

On her blog, Nourishing Days, Shannon shares her pursuit of sustainability, including traditional and fermented food recipes. As a contributing writer for Cultures for Health for the past four years, she has written hundreds of articles and recipes covering nearly every aspect of fermentation. In 2015 she published her first sourdough book, *100% Rye*. Much of her work, personally and professionally, revolves around finding and sharing sustainable ways to feed her growing family.

She lives on a five-acre, off-grid homestead in Texas with her husband, five young children and various farm animals. Her kitchen is almost always a mess.

Index